How to Play
BETTER
FOOTBALL

By C. Paul Jackson
Illustrated by Leonard Kessler

How to Play
BETTER
FOOTBALL

By C. Paul Jackson
Illustrated by Leonard Kessler

Thomas Y. Crowell Company   New York

For all young football strugglers

Manufactured in the United States of America

L.C. Card 72-158707
ISBN 0-690-41567-2

3   4   5   6   7   8   9   10

Contents

1

There Had to Be a Start

You are a mentally and physically healthy boy. You enjoy running and kicking and throwing a football. Add a pinch of crisp autumn weather, and you have the recipe for a football fan and potential football player.

Actually, football has become so popular a sport that today the game is played in almost every kind of weather. No longer is the football season confined to the autumn months. Professional football teams begin practice in July and often play exhibition games before Labor Day. Regular "pro" schedules extend from September to Christmas. The championship playoff games and All Star games carry the football season into mid-January.

Most colleges and many high schools hold spring football practice. Depending on the part of the country you live in, such practices may take place in February, March, April, or May.

Colleges and high schools and leagues of teams made up of boys under high school age usually play regular season schedules that begin in September and end in November. Then come the bowl games, played from Thanksgiving time through Christmas and New Year's.

If you live in a community that has a Pop Warner League, a Midget League, a Boys' League, or any league made up of players under high school age, you may have joined a team or gone to watch games. Almost certainly you have seen pro games or college games on television. You know that when play starts, there are eleven players on each team—always eleven, no more and no less, no matter how many individual players trot on and off the field when play stops.

2

ELEVEN PLAYERS ON A TEAM

Eleven players on a team is one basic of football. Another is that a team has four tries at advancing the ball down the playing field at least ten yards. These tries are called *downs*. If the team with the ball fails to make ten yards in four downs, the ball goes over to the other team. If they do make ten or more yards in four or fewer downs, the team has made a *first down*. They win possession of the ball for another series of downs, and again they must move the ball ten yards or more in four downs or less.

While they have possession of the ball a team is said to be on *offense*. They try to keep the ball until they have taken it across a line in front of them at the end of the playing field. This line is a *goal line*. When they get any part of the ball on or past the goal line, they have scored a *touchdown*.

3

Posts stick up midway between the sidelines, placed either on the goal line for professional teams or on the *end line* ten yards behind the goal line for high school and college teams. These posts are called *goal posts*. A *crossbar* exactly ten feet above the ground connects the *uprights* of the goal posts. If the team with the ball reaches a point where they believe they cannot reach the goal line for a touchdown, they may try to kick the ball through the uprights and over the crossbar to score a *field goal*, which gives them points.

The team that does not have the ball tries to keep its opponents from getting near enough to the goal line to score points either by crossing the goal line or by kicking the ball through the goal posts. They also try to keep the opposing team from making first downs so that they may gain possession of the ball themselves. This team is on *defense*.

Eleven players on each team, downs, goal
lines, goal posts, the scoring of points, offense
and defense—these are the basics of football.
But built on these simple basics, football has
become a very complicated game.

If you have never played football, this book
is for you. You may wonder what goes on in
a football game. This book will answer your
questions and enable you to watch a football
game intelligently. If you have played a little
football—or quite a bit—there are tips that
will help you to become a better player.

The one hundredth birthday of American
intercollegiate football was celebrated in 1969.
There is definite record of a game between
teams captained by William Gummere of
Princeton University and William Leggett of
Rutgers University, played at New Brunswick,
New Jersey, on a windy fall afternoon, November 6, 1869. This was the first American collegiate football game.

But should this game mark the birth of
American football? Voices from the past cry,
"Not so!"

As early as 1827 members of the incoming
freshman class at Harvard University tested
their strength against members of the sopho-

6 more class in a form of football called "bal-lown." The game was held the first Monday of the college year and soon developed into such a free-for-all brawl that the day became known as "Bloody Monday."

Finally in 1860 the Harvard faculty out-lawed Bloody Monday, but by that time games were being played regularly between Boston high schools. The high school contests were not quite as rough as Harvard's ballown, but the point of the game was the same: to move a ball down a field by kicking it.

There is no record of the very *first* game of football ever played, but games in which a ball was advanced toward a goal by kicking were played in Europe long before 1820. To pin-point the beginning of such sport would arouse a larger chorus of "Not so!"

Kicking a ball is enjoyable, and no great stretch of the imagination is needed to visualize a very early beginning of the sport. Picture an early man gathering coconuts for food. He finds one so dried out that no fruit or milk is left inside to eat or drink. He lifts another dried-out coconut and knows from its weight that it too is worthless as food. He might well give the coconut a disgusted kick, the first booting of a "football."

Why is a football sometimes referred to as the pigskin? Could the name have come from the days when men kicked around blown-up

7

8   bladders of pigs during the fall butchering? This was a favorite pastime in colonial days, probably brought to America from England.

Football as we know it today developed from the game of soccer, in which the ball can be advanced toward the goal by kicking or "heading," by using any part of the body *except* the hands or arms. Soccer is still THE GAME in most parts of the world other than the United States and Canada. The story of how the modern game of football came into being turns about a boy named William Ellis.

Playing in a soccer game at the famous boys' school in Rugby, England, Ellis was perhaps startled by the speed of the ball as it soared toward him. Or he may have been annoyed because he was not good at kicking the ball. Instead of heading it, or trapping it preparatory to kicking it, Ellis simply grabbed the ball and ran toward the goal. There were doubtless howls of protest from the opposing team, and probably the run was not allowed. But from then on in England there were two forms of football: soccer, the kicking and heading game, and Rugby—named after the place where it was originated by Ellis—in which the ball could be advanced by carrying.

A plaque in Rugby immortalizes the mo-
mentous deed.

> This Stone
> Commemorates the Exploit of
> WILLIAM WEBB ELLIS
> Who with a fine disregard of the rules of
> Football, as played in his time,
> First took the ball in his arms and ran with it,
> Thus originating the distinctive feature of
> The Rugby Game,
> A.D. 1823

The impulsive run of William Ellis is a far cry from the modern game of football. Over the years men have blended together the characteristics of soccer and Rugby and improved on them, using and sometimes forcing changes in the rules to build the complex game we know today. Every change of rules has had some impact on football. For example, by the turn of the century football in America had become a rough, even a dangerous game. The flying wedge was a popular play, and it depended on brute force. Teammates linked arms

THE FLYING WEDGE

and formed a V-shaped mass that drove down the field in front of the ball-carrier. Many players on the opposing team who tried to break up the flying wedge were seriously hurt.

Upset by the injuries, some people demanded that the game be abolished. It was President Theodore Roosevelt who in 1905 outlawed the flying wedge and probably saved football. The emphasis in the game changed from brute force to speed and cleverness.

In 1906 a change in the rules made the forward pass a legal play, and the game became more open. Other changes in the rules followed as coaches devised new offensive formations. But the change perhaps second in importance to the forward pass in the develop-

ment of our modern game did not come about
until 1945.

H. O. "Fritz" Crisler, then coaching the football players at the University of Michigan, faced a great Army team that year. World War II had not yet ended, and Michigan players of the previous two years were in the armed forces. The West Point players were in training for Army service but still in school. They were mature, experienced football veterans while Crisler's squad was made up largely of physically immature, inexperienced boys who were as yet too young to be in the armed services. So, Crisler came up with a plan to conserve his thin forces. He shuttled players in and out of the game by units, or platoons.

Webster's Dictionary now lists as one definition of platoon: "a group of football players trained for either offense or defense and sent into or withdrawn from the game as a body." Before Crisler platooned his boys against Army, platoon was a word that meant a military unit made up of two or more squads.

Under the platoon system, some boys rest while others play. Before Crisler introduced his system, boys played every minute of the game, on both offense and defense, although coaches did send in substitutes for individual players.

12 The new idea caught fire with coaches, and changes in the rules were made to allow freer substitution and to encourage the use of the platoon system.

Professional teams used the system from the time it came into being. They went even further and introduced special teams who were sent into the game for kicking situations—kickoffs, field-goal tries, and punts—and special teams to receive kickoffs and punts.

But through the years collegiate and high school rules have varied, at times allowing full platooning, partial platooning, and no platooning. One year the rules for high school and collegiate play allowed coaches to make "wild card" substitutions. This meant that full platoons could not be sent into the game, but substitutions for a kicker, passer, or runner could be made at any time.

Platooning allows a coach to play a boy where his skills are most useful. Some boys are better at playing defense; some are weak at defense but excel at carrying the ball, passing, or blocking. Fans like the idea of boys playing where they can best use their skills, and coaches know they can mold better teams when they can use separate units for defense and offense.

Also, every coach likes to provide as much playing time as possible for all the boys on his squad. But platooning does present problems.

One is the rising cost of football equipment. It costs more to buy helmets, protective pads, jerseys, and so forth for the forty to fifty boys who are needed on a team that uses the two-platoon system. Coaches of teams at smaller schools may have trouble finding enough qualified players. If there are not enough boys to make up a defense unit and an offense unit, some boys must "play both ways," must play on both units. Obviously a boy who gets no rest, but is on the field practically every minute of the game, is more likely to be tired and therefore more susceptible to injury.

In spite of the problems, two-platoon football is becoming increasingly popular even at the high school level. No one disputes the fact that the wide-open, exciting, and complex games of today have developed since platoons were introduced to football.

No football player would deny the fact that platoon football makes room for the best skills of the individual to be developed, be he a player in the 95-pound class of a Boys' League or a player on the Number One collegiate team.

2

The Ball, the Playing Field, Equipment, and the Rules

THE BALL

Football has changed a great deal in the years since William Ellis made his famous run. Visiting the campus of a university interested in recruiting him, a fine high school football player stood before a trophy case in the athletic building. Old footballs, marked with the scores of long-past victories, filled the case.

"No wonder the old-timers didn't throw the ball as much as we do!" The boy shook his head. "No one could pinpoint a pass with one of those pumpkins!"

Early footballs, modeled after the Rugby football, were like pumpkins in shape. The rules did not permit a team to advance the ball down the field by throwing it until 1906, and the less pointed the ends, the easier the ball was to kick. Gradually, as the forward pass

14

became a familiar part of the game, rules- makers changed the shape and size of the ball to favor throwing rather than kicking.

Today's football is a sleek, streamlined oval. The distance around the ball from end to end must be no less than 28 inches and no more than 28-1/2 inches. The ball must measure between 21-1/4 and 21-1/2 inches around the middle and must be between 14 and 15 ounces in weight. It must be inflated to between 12-1/2 and 13-1/2 pounds air pressure.

High schools may use either a leather or rubber-covered ball, natural tan in color, with one-inch white stripes. A ball of any other color can be used only if it is approved by both schools.

The football for college games is natural tan color, but a white or colored ball may be used for night games. For day games professional teams use a football of natural tan color and for night games a brown ball with white stripes.

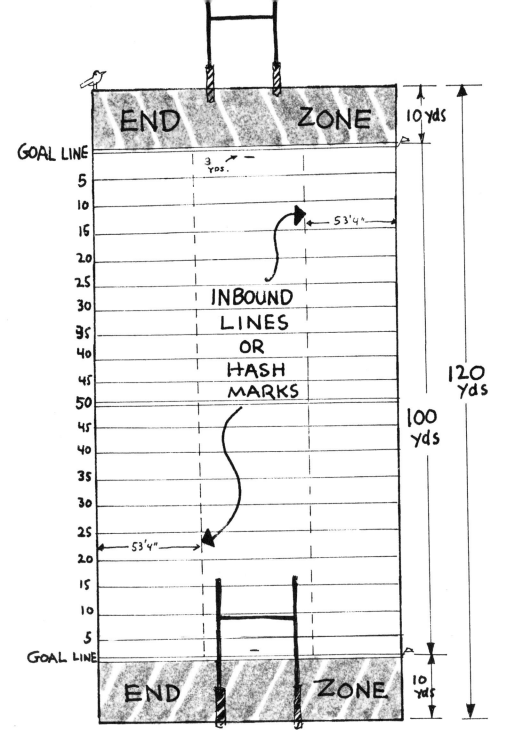

Football fields today vary greatly, ranging from vacant lots with no seats for spectators to beautifully tended playing surfaces in vast stadiums seating tens of thousands of people. But as the boy from a small high school, where the playing field was little more than a pasture with a few broken-down bleachers, said when asked if he was awed by his first game in a large stadium:

"Why, no! The field here is exactly the same size as the one back home. I'm sure I can throw the ball just as far and just as straight here."

The standard playing field for football is a rectangle 120 yards long by 53-1/3 yards wide. The goal lines are 100 yards apart. These are the lines teams try to cross with the ball or to protect from being crossed, depending on whether they are attacking or defending the goal.

Areas extending beyond each goal line to the end line form the *end zones*. This is where *touchdowns* and *safeties* and *touchbacks* are made. When a team on offense gets the ball into the end zone with the ball legally in possession of one of the offensive players, a touchdown is made and scores six points. However, when a

18 player is caught in his own end zone in possession of the ball, it is one of two things—a *safety* or a *touchback*. If the force that carried the ball over the goal line came from a member of his own team, a safety is made and two points are scored for the opponents. If the force that carried the ball over the goal line came from an opponent, it is a touchback, the ball is put in play on the 20-yard line, and no points are scored.

On both sides of the field are lines that run from one end line to the other. These are called *side lines*. End lines and side lines themselves are *out of bounds,* as are areas beyond them, and the ball cannot be moved legally down the field on or outside of these lines. Teams must advance the ball toward either goal line *inbounds*.

QUARTERBACK

53

1

QUARTERBACK
IS FORCED
INTO END ZONE

2

AND IS TA
A SAFET

The playing field between the two goal lines is marked every 5 yards by lines that go from side line to side line and that are parallel to the goal lines. Crossing each of these 5-yard lines are two broken lines drawn from goal line to goal line. These are *inbounds lines*—more commonly known as "hash marks"—and they divide the playing field into three equal zones. When a play ends out of bounds, or between the inbounds lines and the near side line, the ball is placed even with the nearest hash mark for the next play. Bringing the ball out to the hash marks means that neither team will ever need to run a play from a cramped location too close to a side line.

Playing fields for teams whose players are below junior high age may be—and probably should be—shorter than the standard field, 80 yards instead of 100 yards between the goal lines. This does not mean that games between younger boys are not played on regular playing fields. Often no other facilities are available.

Three yards in from each goal line is a short line in front of the goal posts that marks where the ball is placed for the *conversion try* or *try-for-point* after touchdowns. Teams always have one chance to earn extra points after they score

20　touchdowns. They can run with the ball over the goal line or complete a forward pass in the end zone. Or they can kick the ball through the goal posts by place kick or drop kick, though not by a punt.

As of this writing, high school and college rules award one point for a successful kick and two points for a run or a completed pass into the end zone. Professional rules award only one point for a successful try-for-point no matter how the conversion effort is made.

When he tries for an extra point, the kicker aims his kick between the uprights and over the crossbar of the goal posts. The pros use a goal post with a single post behind the goal line but with a crossbar exactly even with the goal line.

SCORING

TOUCHDOWN	6 POINTS
FIELD GOAL	3 POINTS
SAFETY (POINTS TO OPPONENT)	2 POINTS
POINTS AFTER T.D.	
1. BY RUSHING	2 POINTS
2. BY KICKING	1 POINT

Many football people think high schools and colleges should place their goal posts on the goal lines too instead of on the end lines. Successful field goals, which are worth three points, are scored when during the game a player kicks the ball from some point on the field through his opponents' goal post, above the crossbar or directly over one of the uprights. A number of coaches would like to see high school and college teams use field goals more often as scoring weapons, and they probably would if the goal posts were 10 yards closer than they are now to the main part of the playing field.

Professional teams kick field goals regularly during games and even hire players who do almost nothing else but try for this three-point score and the one-point score after touchdowns. Sometimes pro kickers make field goals as far from the goal posts as the 50-yard line, or more rarely, even farther.

21

EQUIPMENT

No player should ever take part in games, scrimmages, or practices without wearing full and proper equipment. Taking things from the top, the helmet is the most important piece of equipment. It provides proper protection for the head—the nerve center of the body—as well as for the face and jaw. The helmet should be made of tough fiber or plastic and be of the "head-suspension type." This means that it should have an arrangement of webbing or strap-type material inside it that provides a cushion of space between head and helmet to

KNEE PADS

22

absorb shock. The face guard should be non-metallic. Material other than metal—usually plastic—absorbs hard impact and lessens the jar while still protecting the jaw and face. A chin strap, detachable at least on one end, holds the entire helmet firmly to the head. Teeth protectors, while separate from the face guard, are a "must" for game play, scrimmage, and all contact drills.

Shoulder pads need to be more than padding. To protect the shoulders properly from hard contact, they should be guards made of corrugated plastic or rugged fiber and lined with shock-absorbing material. Underarm straps should be adjustable.

Football players injure their knees perhaps more than any other part of their bodies. Knee pads need to be durable and shock-absorbing —and carefully fitted.

The younger player can do himself permanent injury by playing hard-tackle football in the backyard, a vacant lot in the neighborhood, or anywhere, for that matter, without good protective equipment. If you do not have a helmet with face guard, a teeth protector, and shoulder and knee pads, then make tag football or touch football the game rather than regular tackle football.

23

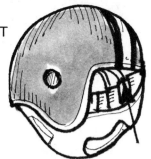

HELMET

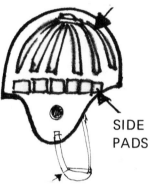

SUSPENSION STRAPS

SIDE PADS

CHIN STRAP

FACE GUARDS

TEETH PROTECTOR

HIP PAD

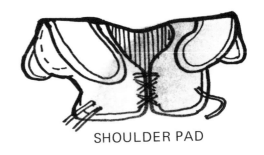

SHOULDER PAD

To more or less ignore hip, kidney, and thigh pads is another mistake young players often make. They are essential in regular football games, practice scrimmage, or anytime you are going to engage in contact drills. They should be made of a tough material, too, and constructed as well as shoulder guards, and should be lined with shock-absorbing material.

Football is a rough, tough game. Nobody who loves football wants it to be any other way, but unnecessary risk of injury should not be taken. Serious accidents often happen when tackle football is played without proper equipment. Don't do it.

Many boys, cautioned not to play tackle football without pads and a helmet, do not always remember or heed warnings. Say a young player wearing no real equipment—only sweatshirt, jeans, and sneakers—tackles a ball carrier bigger than he. A broken collarbone, perhaps a shoulder separation severe enough so that any future football activity is extremely doubtful, may easily result.

Football footwear has changed greatly in the past and may change even more in the future. Some coaches and trainers recommend low-cut shoes in the interest of gaining a tiny fraction of speed through carrying lighter weight. Others want their players to wear shoes with high uppers, which give greater support to the ankle. Another school of thought is that low-cut shoes help to build stronger ankles because the muscles and ligaments and tendons are strengthened through greater use. The best thing to do is to follow the advice of your coach.

Everyone agrees that absorbent, undyed socks should be worn.

Professional, college, and high school players have worn shoes in the past with rather long cone-shaped cleats. Such cleats provide firm footing, but people have begun to suspect that they help to cause knee injuries. The cleats anchor the foot in the ground, and the joint between the upper and lower leg cannot absorb the shock of a driving block or tackle. The National Federation of State High School Athletic Associations decided that "beginning with the 1971 season the maximum length of cleats will be 1/2 inch."

NEW SHOE WITH
SHORTER CLEATS

26 The use of artificial turf is becoming more popular for football fields. Some type of short cleat—the kind used on soccer shoes, for example—works much better on the synthetic fields. The cleats must be short because there is not as much turf for them to dig into as there is on natural ground.

Whatever type of upper or cleat you choose, or your coach recommends, it is of prime importance that the shoe fit.

Every piece of equipment must fit the player. A helmet that is too big or too small may come off just at the very moment you need it most. A ball carrier, blocker, or tackler who loses a shoe at a crucial time is certainly hampered, and not being able to make the right play might cost his team the game.

YOUR EQUIPMENT MUST FIT PROPERLY!

The game of football, like all other games, must be played according to the rules. It is doubtful if there has ever been a referee who would accept an "I didn't know that was against the rules" excuse. A player who breaks the rules and is detected by an official must suffer the penalty, and the penalty usually costs his team more than it costs himself.

There is not space in this book to list the official rules. From time to time rules will be set down and explained when needed. The coach of your team may have copies of the rules available and hand them around to all his players. If not, any good sporting goods store can supply rule books—often at no cost if a sporting equipment manufacturer has printed them for advertising purposes.

Study the rules. Understand what can be done legally and what will cost penalties. A sure way to have a clearer understanding of the calls officials make during a game is to know the rules.

Respect for the rules and for the men who make the calls in a game mark the real football player. Officials are human and they *do* make mistakes. But if there seems to be a reason to

28 question a decision, the wise player lets the coach do the arguing.

A penalty can rob the whole team of hard-won yardage. Penalties often ruin scoring opportunities and sometimes cancel out scores already made. Suppose a pass receiver works and works and finally outmaneuvers the defensive man who is covering him and gets into the end zone all alone. The quarterback throws a perfect pass and the ball is caught. That should be a touchdown and put six points on the scoreboard for your team—but wait!

An official upfield has thrown down a penalty flag against a player on your team. The captain of the other team, the offended team, now has a choice of "taking the gain or the penalty."

OFFICIAL SIGNALS A PENALTY

The referee will carefully and fully explain the choices open to the captain. If he takes the penalty, the ball will be brought back to the spot on the field where the foul was made—or to the yard line from which the ball was put in play if the rules say that the penalty be marked off from that point—the penalty assessed and the down played over. Or, if the captain of the other team decides not to accept the penalty, the ball will be left where it was at the close of the play and the down will count.

If your team had gained few or no yards on the play, the captain might not accept the penalty. He would not want to give you another down or chance to move the ball. But do you think any captain in his right mind would refuse the penalty when your team has scored a touchdown? He would accept it, the touchdown would be erased, and the down would be played over.

A hard-playing aggressive player cannot expect to avoid penalties completely, but he will draw far fewer when he knows the rules and obeys them to the best of his ability.

3

The Players and the Game:
Whites vs. Reds

Suppose you go out for the team in your city
or town at the beginning of the football season
and you become a member of the squad. Your
coach drills and drills and drills his players,
teaching all of you the basic skills. You practice blocking, which is keeping an opponent
from reaching your ball carrier—within the
rules. You practice tackling, which is stopping
an opponent with the ball from advancing
toward your goal—within the rules.

Finally, after several weeks, you are ready
for the first scrimmage or practice game.
Coaches know that no amount of drills will
prevent players from making mistakes under
pressure. So before the regular season starts,
they like to see how well their team performs
in a real game situation. We will watch one
30 twelve-minute quarter of the scrimmage, but

first let's see about the names of the individual **31**
players and their positions on the field.

You probably know that the offense and defense face each other across either side of an imaginary line called the *line of scrimmage*. Actually there are two lines of scrimmage. The scrimmage line for each team runs across the field parallel to the goal line and through the point of the football nearest the team's goal line when the ball is placed in position ready for play. The space between the two lines of scrimmage is known as the *neutral zone*.

The rules say that at least seven of the eleven men on the offensive team must be on or within a foot of this line when the ball is put in play, and of course there may be more than seven. These players form a "front wall" called the *line*. In the middle is the *center*. On each side of him is a *guard*, known as left guard and right guard, depending on which side of the center he plays. Next to the guards are the *tackles,*

THE FRONT WALL

END   TACKLE   GUARD   CENTER   GUARD   TACKLE   END

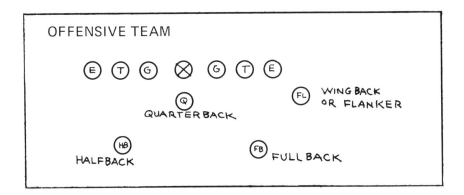

OFFENSIVE TEAM

QUARTERBACK

WING BACK OR FLANKER

HALFBACK

FULL BACK

left and right, and beyond the tackles are the *ends*, left and right.

Guards and tackles are always blockers, and after he snaps the ball, puts the ball in play, the center also becomes a blocker. Ends, too, have blocking duties when they do not go downfield as pass receivers.

Behind this seven-man line are four players in the backfield. The *quarterback* plays behind the center and usually takes the ball from him at the beginning of a play. Traditionally the three players behind the quarterback were the two *halfbacks*, one on his left and one on his right, and the *fullback*, a player standing in between and a little behind the two halfbacks. Sometimes one halfback is positioned wide outside the end, closer to the side line than usual, and is called a *wingback*. Sometimes a back is placed deep behind the quarterback, farther behind him than usual, and is known as a *tailback*.

32

Today, although four players make up the backfield, the names of the positions are changing. The quarterback still takes the ball from center in most plays. But instead of halfbacks and a fullback, we sometimes have two *running backs*—really a halfback and the fullback. Their main job is the same as the one halfbacks and fullbacks have always held: to carry the football on running plays. The fourth man in the backfield is called a *flankerback* or *flanker,* and his principal duty is to receive passes.

The names of the two ends vary also. Instead of left and right end, today's ends are often called *split end*—because he is "split" away from the line and stands a certain distance from his tackle—and *tight end,* because he lines up close to his tackle. No matter what the names of the positions are, though, the basic seven-man line and four-man backfield remains.

SPLIT END   TIGHT END

34   The eleven defensive players may be arranged on the field in any pattern the coach chooses. Some defensive formations use four men in the front line. Others use five or six men. There can be any number up to and including eleven. Basically, however, there is a front wall of defensive linemen and players behind them known as defensive backs.

The names of the defensive positions were once the same as those on the offense, except that the quarterback played very deep, far behind the line of scrimmage, and was known as a safety. Today, the defensive linemen are still called guards, tackles, and ends, although in four-man front walls there are only tackles and ends, the center and guards being replaced by *linebackers.* Two *cornerbacks* and two *safeties* make up the defensive backfield.

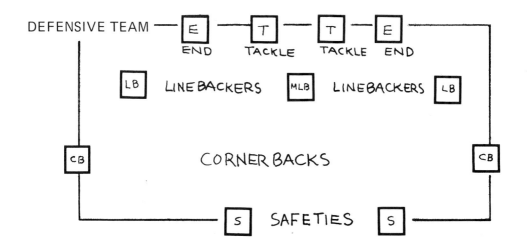

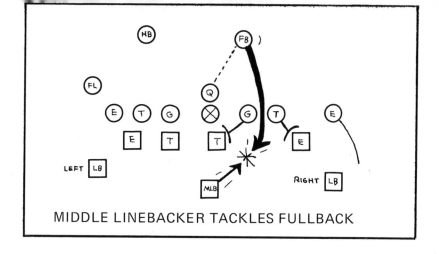

MIDDLE LINEBACKER TACKLES FULLBACK

The *linebackers* play immediately behind the linemen and their chief function is to stop running backs who get past the front wall. As we shall see later, linebackers are also responsible for covering pass receivers in certain game situations. Behind the linebackers come the secondary backs called cornerbacks. They are expected to stop ball carriers who evade the linebackers and to cover pass receivers who are running downfield to catch short or medium-long throws from the quarterback.

The third or tertiary line of defense is the last resort. These deep defensive backs are known as safeties, and they are expected to stop any opponent with the ball who has gotten past the linebackers and cornerbacks, and to cover pass receivers coming down the field for a long pass—a "bomb."

35

36 As you can guess, the players do not line up helter-skelter on the field, with the four men in the offensive backfield standing anywhere they like behind the line and the defensive players scattered haphazardly. Every team practices *formations* or patterns in which each player is assigned a certain position on the field and certain duties to perform. There are defensive formations as well as offensive formations.

From offensive formations *plays* are run. Plays are simply maneuvers in which the actions of each player are coordinated so that teams can work together smoothly to advance the ball down the field.

Every team practices formations and plays, and in the chapters that follow we will be talking about the many types of offense and defense. For now, it is enough to know that when teams take the field for game-play or for game-type scrimmage, they will line up and move in different patterns, all of them planned with one goal in mind: to win.

Now with qualified officials on hand, with the players ready on the side lines, and the cheerleaders yelling for support from the fans in the stands, the game is about to begin.

The first team offense unit and second team defense unit wear red; the first team defense and second team offense wear white. The Red team is to be the visiting team. The field captains of the two teams meet with officials in the center of the field for the *toss of the coin*. The visiting team captain always calls the toss. The referee flips a coin into the air and the Red team captain calls the toss correctly. The referee explains that he may select one of two privileges:

(1) whether his team will kick off or receive the ball;

(2) which goal his team will defend.

The White captain will choose between the options of the privilege not chosen by the winner of the toss.

38   Usually a team wants possession of the ball and the chance to "get their offense rolling" right at the start of the game. So the winner of the toss most often elects to receive the kickoff, the kick that puts the ball in play. Sometimes, though, a coach will instruct his captain to choose the second privilege—which goal his team will defend—instead of the first. If the weather is bad, for example, a coach may want to put his opponents in position on the field at the start of a game so that they face a stiff wind, snow, sleet, driving rain, or perhaps strong sunlight as they try to move the ball toward the end zone. He will then tell his captain that if he wins the toss, he should choose to defend the goal that will give his team the weather advantage.

Today there is no weather advantage, and the Red captain elects to receive the ball. The teams line up for the kickoff.

White team players stretch across the field between their 35- and 40-yard lines. The kickoff to start each half of the game—and those that come after the scoring of a touchdown or a field goal—are made from any point on the 40-yard line between the inbounds lines, unless the ball is moved forward or back because of a penalty.

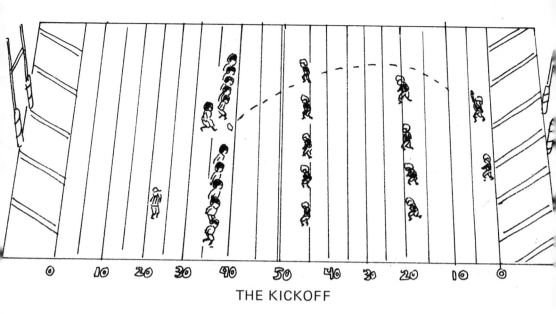

THE KICKOFF

No player on the kicking team—the Whites—may advance past his 40-yard line until the kicker's foot actually comes in contact with the ball. If any player does so, his team will be declared *offside* by an official. Offside carries a penalty of 5 yards.

At least five players on the receiving team, the Reds, must line up across the field ahead of their 45-yard line. They cannot move in back of the 45 until the ball is kicked, or their team will be ruled offside. Other players of the receiving team place themselves anywhere on the field they choose, behind the 45-yard line.

Now the referee blows his whistle, signaling that the game can begin. The kicker starts his run toward the ball.

39

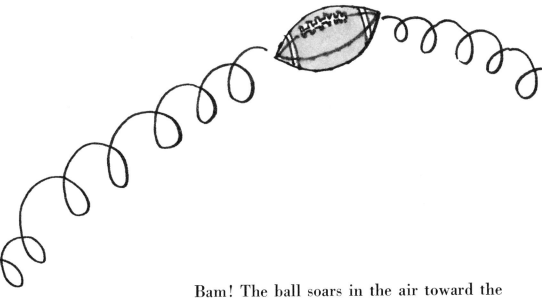

Bam! The ball soars in the air toward the corner of the playing field. The kick is a good one, high and deep. It allows members of the kicking team time to tear downfield and be ready to tackle the man who receives the ball before he can gain much yardage.

A Red halfback receives the ball. He catches it inches short of the goal line and starts up-field. He gets only to the 17-yard line before White tacklers smother him. But back at the midfield stripe, the 50-yard line, an official has thrown down his flag. Something is wrong.

The officials talk briefly, then the referee signals that a White lineman was ahead of the kicker on the kickoff. He was offside.

It is up to the captain of the Red team to decide whether to take or refuse the penalty. If he refuses it, the ball will be put in play on the 17-yard line where his teammate was tackled. The Red team will have to move the ball 83 yards to the White goal line to score a touchdown. If he takes the penalty, the White team will have to kick off again, this time from the 35- instead of the 40-yard line. Hoping that his team can do better running the ball back on a second kickoff, he elects to take the penalty.

No official's flag is thrown this time. The kick is not as high or as deep, and the receiver carries the ball to the Red 36-yard line before being tackled. The Red team is much closer to the White goal line than before. They have good field position.

The Red players form a *huddle*, gathering together around their quarterback behind the line of scrimmage to talk about the next play. Huddles were first used in football games by the offense so that the team could hear what the quarterback was saying. Today the defense uses the same sensible procedure, and in the White players' huddle, the defensive captain is giving instructions about what formation they will use on the next play.

The Red quarterback tells his teammates that the first play will be a pass. He also tells them what number, in the string of numbers he will call at the line of scrimmage, is the *snap signal*. When his teammates hear that number, they know that the center will hand back or snap the ball to the quarterback and the play will begin.

They trot away from the huddle, line up at scrimmage, and the ball is snapped. Taking it, the quarterback steps backward from the line. The ends and backs head down the field, maneuvering to get open, to get in the clear, to get away from the defensive players assigned to

cover them and to be ready to catch the quarterback's throw. The quarterback scans the field. He wants to pick out the receiver who is in the best position to take the pass. He sees a teammate running behind the defensive man who is supposed to cover him. A long spiral pass bores through the air, and the receiver gathers in the ball. He races into the end zone unhampered by the desperate tackle try of a safety man. The Red team has scored a touchdown on the first play from scrimmage!

The receiver ran 32 yards after catching the ball. Altogether the pass and run covered 64 yards of the field.

43

The try-for-point after touchdown—sometimes referred to as the PAT—is a kick. The center snaps the ball to a holder who is crouched on one knee. He places the ball quickly on end for the kicker. The Red PAT soars between the uprights and over the goalpost crossbar, and the scoreboard shows Reds, 7; Whites, 0.

The rules say that a kickoff must follow a score. The team against which a touchdown has been scored has a choice of kicking or receiving the kickoff. The Whites choose to receive. They return the ball only to their 19-yard line, though. Their quarterback calls a running play, sending a back around the left end of the line of scrimmage. But the Red defenders do their basic job perfectly. They keep the offense from advancing the ball.

44

Their end hand fights a blocker and forces the ball carrier to keep running wide toward the side line. Another Red player, a defensive back in the secondary, refuses to allow the White man with the ball to "turn the corner," to get around the end of the line and start his run downfield toward the goal line. When he tries to swerve sharply away from the side line and back toward the center of the field, another defensive back tackles him. The play gains barely a yard.

In the next two plays the White team gives the ball to one of its runners, but they are able to move the ball only 3 yards more. Now it is fourth down, and they will have to gain 6 yards for a first down. This is a kicking situation. The White team will have to *punt*.   **45**

46 The White team has already used up three of its four downs. The yardage they still need for a first down is more than they can reasonably expect to make on the next and last down. If they try to gain the 6 yards and fail, they will have to give up possession of the ball to the Red team at whatever point on the field the ball is when the play ends. This would mean that the Red team would be too close for comfort to the White team's goal line. So normally teams use their fourth down to punt the ball toward their opponent's goal, thus putting them farther away from the end zone they must reach to score. The object of a punt is to put the ball as deep as possible into the territory of the opponent without kicking the ball over the goal line.

Of course the Red player who receives the punt *might* run the ball back for long yardage, even all the way down the field for a touchdown. But more often than not he will be tackled after he has made only a short-yardage return. And he *might* fumble the kick, or fumble the ball when tackled, and a member of the kicking team might recover the fumble for a long gain.

In the huddle the White quarterback calls a punt. The White kicker stands 13 yards be-

hind his center. The other backs are close to
the line, ready to block Red players who will
be charging in to hurry the punt, perhaps to
try to block it. Taking the center's snapback,
the punter steps forward and drops the ball
so that his kicking foot connects with the ball
before it hits the ground.

The Red receiver takes the punt at his own
36-yard line. He tries to evade tacklers by running wide, toward the side line, and is forced
out of bounds at the Red 41-yard line.

FORCED OUT OF BOUNDS

Now the Red quarterback calls a running
play, a smash off-tackle. The ball carrier will
try to slant through a gap between the tackle
and end instead of trying to go around the end
of the line as the White back did earlier.

The quarterback takes the snap from the center and moves backward, pretending he is going to pass. Then he hands the ball off to his fullback. A linebacker stops the fullback after a short 2-yard gain. The Red quarterback calls a pass play.

The captain of the White defensive unit guesses correctly that the play will be a pass, though. His teammates cover the Red pass receivers while the linemen rush hard toward the quarterback.

Sometimes it is better for the passer to "eat the ball" in this situation. This means that he tucks the pigskin close to his abdomen and allows himself to be tackled for a loss rather than risk throwing a pass which might be intercepted, caught by his opponents. But the Red quarterback thinks he can avoid taking a loss by passing the ball to one of his backs who is running toward the side line just behind the line of scrimmage. He does not see that a player

on the other team, a White linebacker on that

side of the field, is carefully watching the back.

The quarterback throws the ball under pressure. The charging linemen are about to tackle him. As a result, the ball is not thrown well. The linebacker darts across and picks off the poor pass as the Red running back lunges toward the ball. An *interception*.

Once he is past the Red back, the interceptor seems to be in the clear for an all-the-way run for a touchdown. But the Red quarterback is faster than the White linebacker. He catches the White player at the 5-yard line and his jarring tackle knocks the ball from the interceptor's grasp.

A *fumble*. It is a free ball which belongs to any player who can grab it. A Red player dives at the ball but it squirts from beneath him. A White player flings himself on it, curls it into the protection of his arms, legs, and abdomen. It is the White team's ball on the Red 4-yard line. The White team has to move the ball only a few yards to score a touchdown.

49

50   On the first play the White fullback runs directly into the line. Red defenders stop him cold for no gain. The White team tries another smash at the middle of the line, and when the officials untangle arms, legs, and bodies, the ball is 2 yards short of the goal line. The last two plays have shown that the Red defense is very tough. Trying to fool them on the next play, the White quarterback calls a third-down pass.

The pass play seems to catch the Red defenders off-balance, and a receiver is open in the end zone. Then, just as the White quarterback releases the ball, his receiver is suddenly not open. A defensive back dashes across in front of him at the last instant, dives, and manages to knock the ball away just before the receiver can grab it. An incomplete pass. The ball returns to the line of scrimmage and the down is lost.

INCOMPLETE !

Now it is fourth down, and still the White
team has 2 big yards to go for a touchdown. A
player in white runs onto the field from the
side line. He is carrying instructions from the
coach.

The Whites line up in kick formation, with
a holder back on the 10-yard line, the kicker
a step and a half behind him. The snapback
comes from center, and the holder places the
ball on end. The kicker steps forward, swings
his leg, and booms the ball over the crossbar.
A *field goal*. The White team has three points.
The score is Reds, 7; Whites, 3.

The kickoff is high and into the end zone.
It is the Reds' ball on their own 20-yard line.

In three plays the Red team moves the ball
only 7 yards, and on the fourth down they
punt. The kick is high and short. The White
receivers see that the Red defenders are almost
on top of them by the time the ball is within
reach. If a White player tries to run back the
punt, he will probably be tackled seconds after
he catches the ball and he may fumble it away.
So instead of trying to run it back, the White
receiver holds one hand high above his head,
signaling for a *fair catch*. This gives him the
right to make the catch without being hit by a

tackler. A player making a fair catch cannot run with the ball after he grabs it, though.

The White receiver takes the ball on his own 48-yard line. His team is in good field position, but the White offense makes only 6 yards in three plays. Their punter gets off a fine kick, which lands on the Red 12-yard line and rolls out of bounds at the 4.

Three Red running plays gain only 8 yards. Their punter stands 2 yards into his own end zone to make his punt. The White left end slips past the man assigned to block him and races toward the kicker. He leaps across the path of the ball and his hands reach it an instant after the ball leaves the kicker's foot. A *blocked punt.*

52

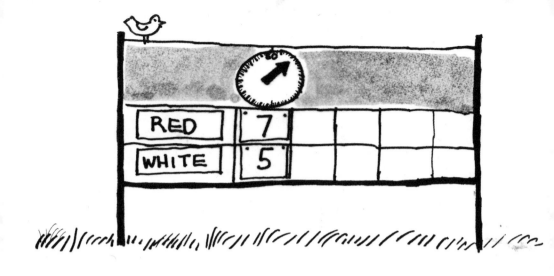

The ball bounces into the end zone, and two White players and the Red kicker dive for it. A red jersey is curled around the oval when the referee unscrambles the pile. A *safety*.

The force that carried the ball over the goal line came from the snapback and the kicker's foot. Two points scored for the White team. The score is 7–5 now. The Reds kick off from their 20-yard line.

Neither team can make a first down during the rest of the period, and the score at the end of the first quarter is Reds, 7; Whites, 5.

It has been a good quarter of play. Coaches saw things to be proud of and things that showed need of more work on both the offense and defense. But all in all, it was a good quarter of play.

53

4

Team Offense:

Plays and Formations

When they are in possession of the ball, all football teams have one main goal: to move the ball down the field and to score points. In the Red vs. White scrimmage in the previous chapter you watched each team advance the ball in several different ways, and if you had watched the rest of the game you might have seen a few more.

You saw the teams run with the ball. *Running plays* may send the ball carrier smashing directly into any spot in the defensive line or carrying the ball around one end of the line or the other. Of course receivers of kickoffs and punts are also advancing the ball by running when they carry it back up the field.

Teams can *pass* the ball to move it down the field. When the ball is thrown toward the opponents' goal, a *forward* pass is made. A legal forward pass must be thrown from within or behind the neutral zone.

The ball may also be thrown directly to either side of the field or backward at any time and as many times during a play as a team wants. Such tosses are called *lateral passes*.

As we have seen, teams can also use *kicks* as offensive weapons, gaining ground on exchanges of punts.

And finally, *penalties* may help the offense. Called against defensive players, penalties gain yardage for the offense. For example, suppose a defensive player charges across the line of scrimmage before the offensive center snaps the ball. He will be ruled offside, which calls for a penalty of 5 yards. The ball will be moved 5 yards closer to the goal line the offensive team is attacking. It is perfectly legal for a quarterback to change the usual rhythm of his signal calling, making his count longer. Sometimes quarterbacks do this, hoping to catch a defensive player off guard and cause him to charge across the neutral zone too soon. However, teams do not rely on penalties as part of their game strategy. In fact, the best way for a team to move the ball down the field is to be in condition to "whip its opponents physically," to carry out blocking assignments properly so that the ball carriers and pass receivers can do their jobs.

Today running and passing are the two most commonly used offensive weapons. Football would be a much simpler game if every team used only one kind of running play or even *all* running plays, or one kind of passing play or even *all* passing plays.

Though if the same player carried the ball on running plays, and if he always headed for the same spot in the line, the defense would quickly learn what to expect. They would arrange their men on the field in such a way that they could easily "gang" tackle the ball carrier before he really got going. Every defensive player could concentrate on tackling the single runner to the ground.

DEFENSE "GANG" TACKLES BALL CARRIER

On the other hand, suppose the defense did not have to worry about running plays. Suppose they could be sure every play was going to be a pass. The defensive backs would cover only the pass receivers, and the linemen would be able to rush the passer on every play.

So coaches make up and teach their teams a number of different plays so that the defense can never be sure what form of attack is coming next. Some teams have so many different plays in their play book that a young player feels he will never learn all of them. "We have umpteen running plays—line smashes, off-tackle slants, sweeps, and reverses. We have a million passing plays, with receivers running downfield in a zillion different patterns. I wish we used just three running plays and two passing plays!"

The young man is not likely to get his wish. Football is a complicated game, and while it is true that how well any one play is executed is more important than surprising opponents with a move they do not expect, coaches come up with new plays and variations of old plays all the time.

In any play each member of the team has a job to do in order to make the play work. Line

58   smashes, off-tackle slants, sweeps, traps, reverses, and draw plays: these are all running plays. They are maneuvers in which a ball carrier—usually one of the running backs—tries to advance the ball down the field, and they are successful only when every player carries out his blocking assignment. When a ball carrier cracks directly into the interior line of the defense—the area along the line of scrimmage between the two tackles—the play is called a *line smash* or a *line buck*.

On an *off-tackle slant* the ball carrier moves diagonally, in a slanting direction, from his position in the backfield toward the gap between the tackle and the end. The play may go either to the right or left side of the line.

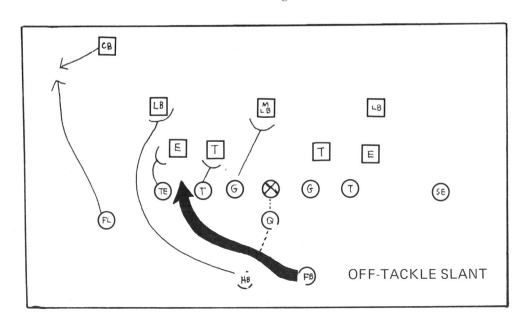

OFF-TACKLE SLANT

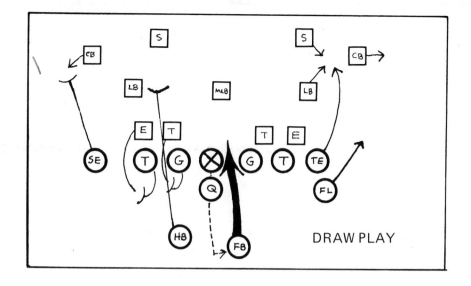

DRAW PLAY

An offensive lineman sometimes takes advantage of an opponent's charge, allowing him to cross the line of scrimmage and pass through or penetrate the "front wall." A blocker then traps him, blocking him to one side while the ball carrier slams through the hole in the line he has left. This is a *trap* play.

Sometimes the offensive team lines up in such a way that their opponents expect a passing play. If the defensive linemen are fooled, are "drawn through the line" and head for the passer, they may become victims of a *draw* play. The quarterback hands off quickly to one of his ball carriers. The defensive men are charging too hard toward the passer to be able to change direction easily, and the ball carrier rams past them into the secondary.

59

60 There are other running plays in which the path of the ball carrier is less direct, in which he follows a longer route. The advantage is that he can get up a better "head of steam," be going at top speed, and may gain room to maneuver out in the open space. For example, when he runs around one end of the line, or flank as it is frequently called, there are fewer men to be blocked, and blockers have more time to reach the defensive men. The play is known as a *sweep,* an *end run.* If the defensive men can be blocked out or delayed long enough for the ball carrier to get around the flank (called "turning the corner") there is likely to be a sizable gain. This play is so common as to be routine with every offense.

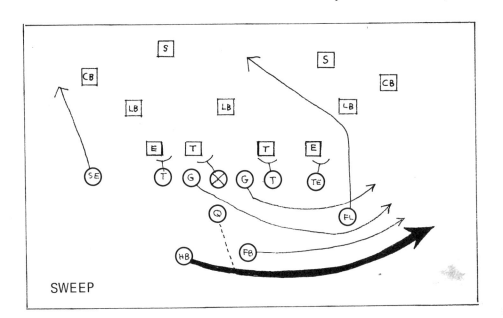

SWEEP

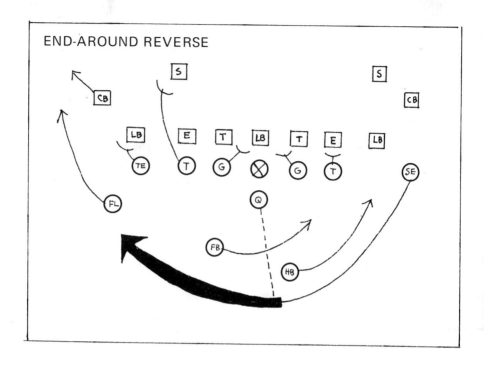

END-AROUND REVERSE

To vary the routine and to try to catch their opponents off guard, teams use plays that start out as if they are going to be sweeps. The quarterback pretends he is handing the ball to a player who heads toward one end of the line as if he is running a sweep. Another player, running in the opposite direction, comes around behind the first player, and the quarterback hands the ball to him. This is known as a *reverse*. Reverses are also routine, but from here coaches build double reverses and triple reverses.

61

New forward-pass plays and new patterns are being introduced all the time. A very common passing play is one in which the ball is thrown to an end running downfield, turning out or in—toward the side line or toward the middle of the field. Another is a pass to an end or flankerback cutting sharply across the defensive backfield just beyond the line of scrimmage. The first is known as a "down-and-out" or "down-and-in" pattern and the second is a "look-in" pass which you have probably seen on television. There are as many differences in the patterns run by receivers as there are receivers. (The various patterns will be discussed in a later chapter.)

Of course the defense does not stand still.

A DOWN-AND-OUT PATTERN

Soon after a new offensive play or formation is shown, the defense will come up with moves to combat it.

A coach of offense knows that any and every play he teaches his team can produce touchdowns *if* each player does his job well. The defensive coach believes firmly that his men can stop any offensive play *if* every defensive man executes his assignment properly. Football is that simple. It comes down to every man on the team doing—or failing to do—his job well.

Any coach, when pinned down, will admit that fancy plays do not guarantee that the ball will be moved. The showdown always comes to what is called execution, the way assignments are carried out. Many kinds of offensive plays have been run from many different formations, then discarded when the defense caught up with them and was able to blunt their effectiveness. Sometimes a rule change makes illegal what has been a fine tool of offense.

For example, Knute Rockne—almost a legendary coach when he was alive and certainly one since his tragic death in a plane crash in 1931—devastated opponents in his time with his famous Notre Dame box formation and hard-hitting, quick and shifting linemen. At that time the rules allowed a player to shift—to change his position—just before the snap of the ball. Notre Dame men shifted around on the field at lightning speed, hitting the weak spots in the defense. Because they were moving when the ball was snapped, they had an advantage over the defensive players. They could hit them with more force than they would have been able to from a stationary position.

Finally the rules were changed. Today, if a player moves to another position after he has taken his initial stance, he must come to a full, one-second stop before the ball is snapped. No more than one back can be in motion until after the snap is made.

Plays are run from formations, as we saw earlier, and since Knute Rockne's time they have change a good deal. Just as coaches have invented a wide variety of plays over the years, they have come up with a number of different formations. Today football people talk of the "Power-I," "Triple Option," "Y-formation," "Wishbone-T," and what have you. They speak of split end, tight end, flankerback, running back, middle guard, linebacker, cornerback, safety, monster man, and rover as positions football players play. Do not be confused by

the number of different formations and the
new names given to old positions. Every offensive formation uses eleven players, no more
and no less. They differ only in the pattern the
players are arranged in on the field.

Originally the eleven men on offense lined
up as in the marginal diagram. In fact, in the
old days the defense used almost exactly the
same alignment, and as we have already seen,
the positions were known by the same names.
The only differences were that on defense the
fullback came in closer to back up the front
line and the quarterback played deeper in the
backfield and was known as the safety man.

Then came an offensive formation in which
the halfbacks and the fullback stood in a row
parallel to the linemen. The quarterback was
still behind the center but closer to him. We
know this now as the basic *T-formation*, but it
was called "backs in line" and other similar
names when it was first used. One of the ad-
vantages of the formation was that the quarterback could get the ball to the ball carrier faster.
The fullback stood closer to him and he could
pitch out to any of his backs for off-tackle plays
and sweeps when he did not hand off the ball
for line bucks. But a disadvantage was that the

PLAYERS LINED UP LIKE
THIS IN THE OLD DAYS

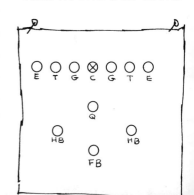

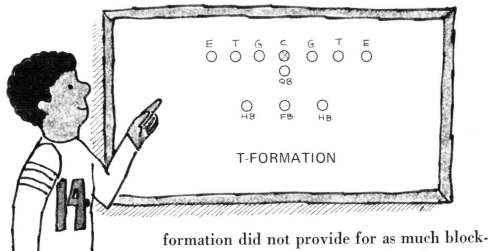

T-FORMATION

formation did not provide for as much blocking in front of the ball carrier. The other backs did not have time to get in front of him.

All coaches like to come up with something new. There are some who pull new formations and plays from their play books the way magicians pull rabbits from their hats.

In one variation of the T-formation known as the *I-formation,* the quarterback and the running backs stand behind the center in a line that is at right angles to the line of scrimmage. A *Power-I* differs from the regular I-formation mostly in blocking assignments. In a *Y-formation* the quarterback and fullback stand directly behind the center forming the tail of the Y, and the two halfbacks stand behind them at the ends of the arms of the Y. As you can see, this is a variation of the T-formation too.

Notice in the diagrams of the *single-wing* and *double-wing* formations that the quarter-

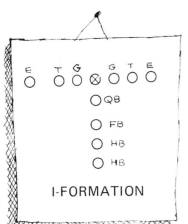

I-FORMATION

back does not stand close to the center. Usually
in these wingback formations the quarterback
does not handle the ball. Instead of handing
the ball back to the quarterback as he does in
the variations of the T-formation, the center
snaps the ball directly to the ball carrier. Before the quarterback became primarily a passer,
in the wingback formations he was a blocker.
Today, even when a wingback formation is
used to diversify the offense, the quarterback
more or less stands around. Coaches do not risk
injury to their passer by subjecting him to the
physical hazards of blocking.

Earlier we spoke briefly of the pro-set formation, in which the split end lines up wide of
the tackle on one side of the line. The other

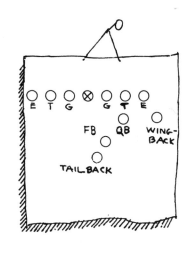

SINGLE-WING FORMATION

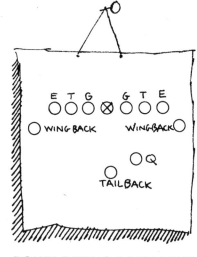

DOUBLE-WING FORMATION

68 end, the tight end, takes position right next to the tackle on the opposite side.

A flankerback lines up at least a yard behind and some distance outside the tight end. Of course a coach may position both ends split wide of the tackles, and in such a case the flanker lines up a yard behind and between the end and tackle, thus becoming a "slot" back.

In the pro-set, the quarterback almost invariably crouches behind the center and handles the ball on all plays except kicks. The set backs—two—are referred to as running backs.

Today more and more teams are using the pro-set formation. However, the T-formation and the single-wing and double-wing are still basic. Teams sometimes use one or more of these three when they find that they cannot move the ball well from the pro-set. Their op-

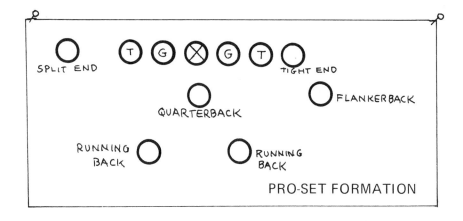

PRO-SET FORMATION

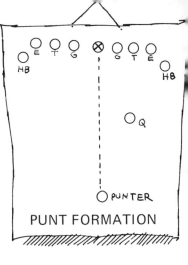

PUNT FORMATION

ponents may be too skilled at defending plays run from the pro-set. When a team uses several formations, they are often said to play "multiple offense."

For punting, all teams use essentially the same formation. Sometime in the future a formation may be invented that will be more effective for punts, but it is difficult to conceive.

As we said before, don't allow the many different formations to confuse you. They are all designed to move the ball against the defense, and if one fails, or if the defense comes up with a formation of its own to stop it successfully, that formation will fall into disuse.

It may be that sheer number of variations of plays and formations could overwhelm a defense. Fifteen or twenty variations of formations *might* confuse a defense, foul them up so that the offense could make yardage easily. However, a defense solidly coached on defensive fundamentals will not be baited by razzle-dazzle offense gimmicks, but will adjust and clobber the fancy stuff.

Championship teams that use comparatively few plays have been produced, but on every play every man was doing his job.

5
Team Defense

In the early days of football the rules were more favorable to the defense, and teams emphasized this part of their game. Most games were low-scoring, and many were won or lost by one touchdown or by a point after touchdown. There are still low-scoring games, even scoreless games, but football has "opened up." Changes in the rules have encouraged teams to use a greater variety of offensive plays. This has given the defense more problems to deal with, and the result now is that the offense scores more points.

Some coaches hold that "the best defense is a strong offense. The other team can't score while you own the football." It is true that the other team will not make touchdowns or field goals while your team has possession of the ball. But a team that slights its defense is asking for trouble. Knowledgeable football peo-

ple believe that an outstanding team must have
a stout defense along with its strong offense.

The rules of the game provide that your opponents will have the ball at least some of the time, no matter how good your offense is. For example, after scoring a touchdown or a field goal, your team must kick off to your opponents. Also, no team can avoid fumbles and pass interceptions once in a while. So it is important that your team be able to keep opponents from scoring when they do get the ball —and that is the name of the defensive game.

Coaches of defense did not exactly sit back and wring their hands in despair when faced with the greater variety of offensive formations and plays. Playing defense today requires as much intelligence, drive, and technique as playing offense. Many coaches will tell you that defense requires *more* of those qualities.

Team defense is like team offense in the sense that both work from basic alignments or formations, which are frequently called "sets." You probably know that there are many different sets. The eleven players on the defensive team do not line up on their area of the field in any position they choose. They are grouped in a specific formation, with certain duties to

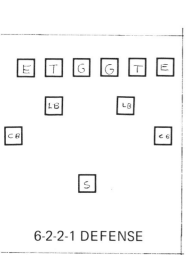

6-2-2-1 DEFENSE

perform and sections of the field to protect. The aim of any defensive set is to combat the different formations of the offense. The sets often change from play to play as the defensive captain decides which play the other team is probably going to use.

Defensive sets are known by numbers such as 6-2-2-1; 6-1-2-2; 4-4-3; 4-3-2-2. Note that the sum of the numbers is always eleven. The numbers tell how many men are in the first or front line and how many linebackers, corner-backs, and safeties there are.

A 6-2-2-1 set worked well and was popular for a long time. In fact, it is still used often by some teams and by all teams on occasion. Two ends, two tackles, and two guards make up the front line. Two players are positioned some-what deeper than the linemen. They are called linebackers and are expected to do just that—back up the line. Two more players are positioned beyond the linebackers and out wider, closer to the side lines, to back up the line-backers and to cover players on the opposing team who may be going to receive passes. These are the cornerbacks. The safety men play deeper than the cornermen and, as we have seen, are the final defenders, expected to stop any opponent with the ball who has gotten

away from all of the other members of the
team.

A six-man line is stronger against running plays than a four-man line would be, simply because there are more men in a good position on the field to tackle ball carriers. But you can see that this set is weak against passing plays. Only three men are in the backfield ready to try to stop players on the other team from catching passes.

The 6-1-2-2 set gives better pass coverage than the 6-2-2-1 set. By using only one line-backer instead of two, it frees a man to guard receivers downfield. The single linebacker, instead of being responsible for one half of the area of the field immediately behind the front line, ranges from one end of the line to the other. Because he moves to wherever he is needed, this defender is called the "rover." Ideally he is the roughest, toughest man playing

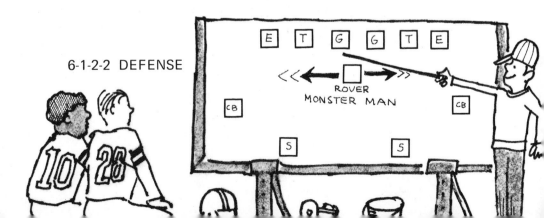

6-1-2-2 DEFENSE

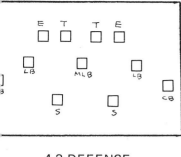

4-3 DEFENSE

defense. Expected to wreck offensive running plays, to become a monster to the offense, he is also called the "monster man."

However, a monster man can be double-teamed. This means that two offensive players are put on him to block him out of the way of their teammate who is running with the ball. Also, one linebacker cannot do as good a job as two or three in defending against running plays or short-distance passes thrown to offensive players just beyond the line of scrimmage. So looking for a better all-around defense, coaches have come up with a set you may hear referred to as the "4-3."

All eleven defensive men are used, of course. The set is also called the 4-3-4 and 4-3-2-2, which it technically is. The 4-3 is a football term which assumes that you know there are four defensive backs supporting the front four linemen and the three linebackers. The four backs, the two cornerbacks and two safeties, all perform the same functions. Their main job is to cover pass receivers, but they also stop ball carriers who have gotten by the defensive linemen and linebackers.

In the 4-3 two big, rugged, hard-charging ends and two tough tackles make up the front

line. You have probably heard sportscasters
refer to these four men with such colorful
terms as "fearsome foursome" or "people
eaters." This front line forms the first wall of
defense against running plays. On passing
plays they lead the rush on the passer. Normally they go after the quarterback while the
linebackers and cornerbacks and safeties pick
up potential pass receivers. But in game situations where the defensive captain is fairly certain that the upcoming play will be a pass, the
defense may "red dog" or "blitz." This means
that the linebackers—and sometimes one or
both safeties, too—join the front four in an
all-out charge at the quarterback. They try to
tackle the passer before he can get the ball
away or hurry him into throwing a poor pass.

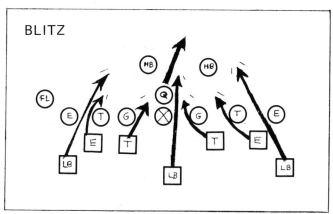

BLITZ

QUARTERBACK "READS" BLITZ AND CALLS A DRAW PLAY

But a blitz can backfire, can work *against* the defense, when the quarterback "reads" the defense and knows they are going to rush him. Sometimes a quarterback is able to guess what the defensive team is going to do because he notices a difference in the posture or stance of one or more of his opponents when both teams line up at scrimmage. Perhaps one defensive player looks especially eager. In the huddle the quarterback has already told his teammates what the next play will be, but he can change the play right at the line of scrimmage before the ball is snapped.

Instead of the passing play he planned to use, he might call a draw play, sending a runner speeding past the blitzers. As we saw earlier, the defensive players are usually charging so hard toward the quarterback that they cannot change direction easily to tackle the ball carrier.

Of course the defense may guess that the
quarterback is calling a new play at the line
of scrimmage. There is nothing to keep them
from changing their plans too, except that they
do not have the time to make any great change.
Also, they cannot be sure that the quarterback
is really changing the plan. He might be trying to trick them. This constant battle of wits
between the offense and the defense is fully as
important as the physical battle.

Rushing the passer is only one of the many
ways the defense tries to force the offense into
giving up possession of the ball. Such things
as delaying and covering pass receivers, making interceptions, forcing and recovering fumbles, and blocking punts are certainly parts of
team defense.

Every defense has formations they use at
special times in the game. For example, there
are sets to be called by the defensive signal
caller when the offense lines up in an out-of-
the-ordinary formation, such as a *spread*. Here,
the offensive linemen are positioned farther
apart from each other than usual and the backs
line up much wider, closer to the side lines
than usual. To the defense, a spread formation means that a trick play, a pass, or a sweep
may be coming. So the defensive set will be

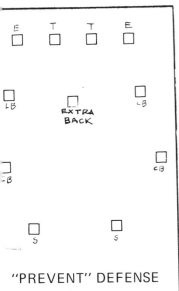

E T T E

LB EXTRA LB
BACK

LB CB

S S

"PREVENT" DEFENSE

very flexible, ready to send defensive strength where it is most needed to meet the offensive threat.

A "victory" or "prevent" defense is used when there are only minutes left to play and the team on defense is ahead. Linebackers drop back from the line of scrimmage, playing more loosely, and cornerbacks play somewhat deeper than usual. The offense may make short gains by running with the ball through the line or by completing short passes. Playing time is being consumed, though. The defense hopes that by covering more fully the part of the field closer to the goal line, they can prevent the *long* pass or *long* run which may score a touchdown in the last moments of the game.

A special goal-line defense is among every team's defensive sets. When opponents have moved the ball to within a few yards of the end zone, the defense may use a front line of eight, nine, or ten men, or linebackers may play so close to the front line that together they form a two-ply wall. The players unite to throw back line smashes or line bucks. Designed to provide "muscle" by bunching defensive players along the line of scrimmage, the goal-line **78** defense is very vulnerable to passes out wide toward the side lines of the field or "basket-ball" tosses just over the line of scrimmage. But when the offensive team is close to the goal line, pass receivers find it much harder to get away from their opponents than they do in the open field. It is almost certain that the other team will try to use a running play, a power play, directly into the line.

Here is a diagram of one goal-line defense. There are of course others. In this set, the defensive halfback—the safeties, really—are set a step deeper than the linebackers as a precaution against a possible pass or a sweep. Once they see that the offense is going to use a line buck, though, these defensive backs also hurl their bulk at the ball carrier.

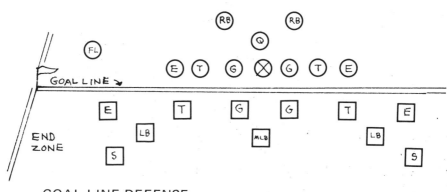

GOAL-LINE DEFENSE

It will be up to your coach to decide what "system" of defense your team will use. One coach, in talking about the problems of defense with the writer, had a novel—if tongue-in-cheek—idea.

"I roomed with a psychologist in college," the coach said. "He has a theory about defense. According to him, the defense of territory is instinctive, handed down to us through the ages. As the threat of an invader coming into your territory gets stronger, your instinctive resistance increases. Also, the invader experiences a form of guilt because he realizes he is the intruder. Thus he may become inept suddenly, which in football could lead to fumbles, misplays that cause penalties and interceptions of passes."

The coach drew a long breath, let it out, and grinned. "Our defense has been so poor lately that maybe we need a resident psychologist to teach us what to do."

Better than a resident psychologist to improve a team's defense is work and work and more work.

6
Blocking and Tackling

In the next chapters we will be talking about individual positions; about how to play center, guard, tackle, end, running back, and quarterback; and about the specialists on football squads. Blocking and tackling, though, are skills every member of the team must learn, no matter what position he plays.

Let's look at both sides of the coin.

If you play on a team with separate offensive and defensive units, you may wonder why you have to learn blocking *and* tackling. You know that blocking is a skill that is used in offensive play, that tackling belongs to the defense. Suppose, though, you are a defensive back, trained to cover pass receivers and to tackle them—or any other ball carrier who comes downfield. Suppose a teammate is nearby when you slam into an opponent with the ball; you jar the ball loose from his grasp when you tackle him, and your teammate recovers the fumble before the ball touches the ground. He can run with it, you know. Or perhaps a teammate intercepts a forward pass. The instant that a defensive man gains possession of a ball that he can legally advance toward the opponent's goal, the defensive team becomes the offensive team. If you have the know-how to block an opposing player who is about to tackle your teammate, you just *may* be the player responsible for your team scoring a touchdown.

On the other side of the coin, suppose you play on the offensive unit. You know that blocking is the way to keep tacklers from reaching your ball carrier. It makes sense to work and work and work to develop your blocking. But why spend time learning and perfecting tackling techniques?

Perhaps it was your teammate who fumbled the ball in the game just described. The instant that a defensive man gains possession of a ball that he can legally advance, *your* offensive unit becomes a defensive team. If you have the know-how to tackle, you *may* be the player who prevents a touchdown from being scored against your team.

Say you are a passer, a punter, or a field-goal

kicker. Your pass may be intercepted, your
kick may be blocked, and the ball recovered
by an opponent. A member of the team receiving the kick may advance the ball, you know.
You may be the only man between your opponent and the goal line. If you have learned how
to tackle, you may save your team a touchdown.

The fact that *every* member of a football
team must develop blocking and tackling skills
is worth repeating.

BLOCKING

Blocking is the art of charging into an opponent and using the body and arms, but *not* the
hands, to drive him away from the path of the
ball carrier. There are many different types of
blocks, but they all fall into two main categories, *line blocking* and *open-field blocking*.

Any player may have occasion to throw
either type of block. A lineman—a guard,
tackle, center, or an end—will most often use
the *shoulder block*, which is the mainstay of
line blocking. But a lineman may be downfield
and in position to help his ball carrier by wip-
ing out a potential tackler. He must be able to
throw a *body block*, which is an open field

block. Backs must know how to use both kinds of blocks too, for often a shoulder block downfield is more effective than the body block backs are most familiar with.

Blocking is crucial in any football game. Your formations and plays may be sound, the ball carriers may be fast and shifty, but your team will not be able to move the ball very far downfield without good blocking. Desire, muscle, staying power, timing, and drive: all these qualities go to make up the good blocker, and many coaches will vote desire as the most important. You must *want* to block. You must relish rugged contact. If you do not like hard, solid "mixing it up," you can never be a really good blocker.

Early aviators used to say that "any landing you can walk away from is a good landing." Football coaches accept any legal block that gets the job done and protects the man with the ball. But there *are* basic techniques to learn that will make you a better blocker.

1. Focus your attention on the tackler you want to block. Look into the block and "through" your target. A leaning block—a block thrown *at* the tackler rather than *through* him—is like a pass thrown without

follow-through. You get most effectiveness only when you block through the target.

2. Aim your block so that your body is always between the opposing tackler and the path of the ball. No matter whether your teammate who is carrying the ball is in the crowded area near the line of scrimmage or running in the open field, your aim is to force the tackler away from your ball carrier's path.

3. Get under the tackler, get leverage on him. If you hit him low enough so that you lift him off his feet, you will find that it is much easier to move him out of the way. An opposing lineman may charge in so close to the ground that you can't get under him. Such a "submarine" charge is best handled by using your weight, bearing down over his head and shoulders, and slanting his charge away from the path of your ball carrier.

4. The feet form the base of a good block. You will not be able to carry through with your block and hold it without solid footing.

The most commonly used block is the shoulder block, and as we have seen, it is the most effective block in line play. Suppose your quarterback has called a running play. As a lineman your job may be to "open a hole" for the ball carrier. This means that you must clear a path for him by throwing a block at the potential tackler and moving him out of the way. The shoulder block is the block to use. Sometimes two linemen, the tackle and the guard, combine to "double-team" an opponent. Each throws a shoulder block on the defensive man, pushing him to one side, and the ball carrier races through the hole in the line.

The shoulder block starts from the three-point stance.

Inexperienced boys often take a stance which throws their weight too far to the front. Such a stance will cause you to lunge when you charge forward and will make it difficult for you to go in any direction other than straight ahead. You will become "easy meat" for your opponent, who will be able to sidestep you or shove you out of his way.

Draw a square on the ground that is about two and one-half feet on a side. Place either foot—depending on which position feels right to you—in one back corner of the square and the other foot on the opposite side of the square, at about the midway point. If your right foot is in the back corner of the square, place your right hand in the front corner on the same side of the square. If your left foot is in the back corner, place your left hand in the front corner on the same side of the square. Adjust your feet to a position where you are most relaxed. If you like, you can move the back foot even with the front one. Some players find they can coil their legs better in this position. This gives them a good spring when they charge toward their opponent.

The knuckles of the hand that is on the ground should be bent so that there is a slight pressure on the first three fingers. You can hold your other hand close to your chest, your forearm resting on your leg, slightly above the knee, on that side of your body. The lower part

POSITION YOURSELF IN A SQUARE

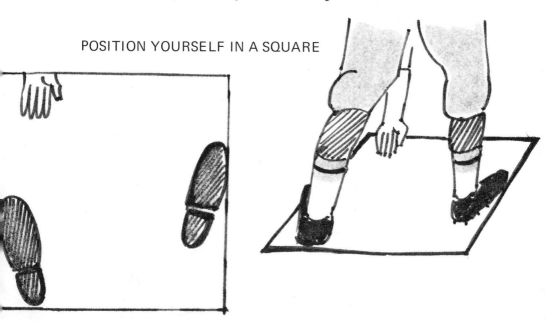

THREE-POINT STANCE

of your legs, your trunk, and head should be perpendicular to the line of scrimmage. *Carry your weight mostly on the inside half of the balls of your feet, your toes pointing out and your heels in.*

Spread your knees as wide apart as your feet. Your shoulders should be level, your back straight and sloping upward from posterior to shoulders. Your head must be up so that you are looking straight ahead.

This is the three-point stance, which allows you to move quickly and easily forward, backward, or laterally, to one side or the other. You can perfect your stance by posing in front of a mirror large enough to reflect your complete image. Face the fellow in the mirror head-on and also look at your stance from both sides, correcting any defects.

A word of caution: if the boy looking back at you is really mean-looking, get out of the way before he charges. You may break the mirror defending yourself!

You can use the shoulder block to move your man backward or to one side or the other, depending on the play. Don't give him any hint with which shoulder you intend to attack, or in what direction you are going to move him. Charge forward and make contact with your shoulder and the side of your neck, your head turned to one side and your feet churn-

SHOULDER BLOCK

ing forward. Once contact is made, maintain it and keep driving.

A player throwing a downfield block is faced with a tougher situation than moving a man in the line. Open-field blocking calls for techniques that are different from line blocking. The man you are to block is out of the heavy traffic around the scrimmage line. He is out in the open where he has freedom to move. Here the *cross-body block* is most effective.

Throw your body across the tackler's thighs so that your head and shoulders are on one side of his legs, your knees on the other. As you make contact with him, snap hard against him, with your hips and upper leg delivering the force of the block. If you do not knock the tackler off his feet, you must try to maintain contact with him. Support yourself on your hands and "crab-walk" against him to keep him off balance. Arch your back to make yourself into as high a fence as possible and keep between the tackler and the path of your ball carrier. This block is frequently called simply a *body block*. Every player uses it at one time or another.

As you approach your man for the block, watch him closely. He may pretend he is going to move away from you in one direction and

CROSS-BODY BLOCK

then run quickly in the opposite direction. Try not to fall for such tricky fakes. You make your hands into fists, bringing both arms up and keeping your elbows out. This gives you more blocking surface with which to engage your opponent in case you cannot get into position for a body block. It is enough if you can keep him out of the way while your ball carrier scoots past.

Remember that the defensive man can use his hands to yank at your shirt or push you out of his way. Use of hands by the blocker—the man on offense—is a foul. So carry your hands near your sides or clutch the front of your

91

jersey so that you are not tempted to use them.

It is usually best not to leave your feet when you throw a block, although when you cannot make contact in any other way, you do so. But warding off a tackler, keeping him away from the ball carrier and out of the play, then going on prepared to make another block is the mark of the superior blocker.

You cannot count on a head-on meeting with the tackler in the open field. Often you will have to block from the side, but you must be careful that "from-the-side" does not slip into "from-the-rear."

Blocking from behind, across the defensive man's legs, is known as clipping and calls for a 15-yard penalty from the spot of the foul. Clips happen most often when the tackler pivots, or changes directions, after a blocker has clearly begun his charge. No blocker—except a dirty player—deliberately clips, because a clip may injure an opponent badly.

In passing and kicking situations, line blocking is different from blocking for running plays. You do not charge toward your opponent as you would if you were clearing a path for the ball carrier. To protect the kicker, to prevent your opponents from breaking through the line for a shot at blocking the kick, or at least hurrying it, offensive linemen form a solid wall.

Blockers come up from the stance in a crouch and maintain tight contact with their opponents. The block is a stationary one. The blockers meet the charge of their opponents, but do not move forward or to either side themselves, except if necessary to keep in front of the defensive man.

To block for the passer, blockers come up from the stance in a crouch and step backward. They form a pocket of protection to keep defense men away from the quarterback until he can get the pass away. Use short, jabbing blocks, recovering after each one to maintain contact with your man. Your job is to keep the quarterback from being harassed, to give men going downfield to receive the pass enough time to break into the open and the quarterback time to pick out the one in best position to receive the pass. This time can be given only if blockers keep the defensive men from reaching the passer.

The blocker who can learn the skills necessary to hold off an aggressive pass-rush is sure to be treasured by his coach. If an opponent gets to the quarterback and forces a hurried pass or deflects the ball, the play is ruined.

94 Blockers *must* keep defense men from reaching the passer.

There are other blocks used in different situations in games: pivot blocks, sideswipe blocks, check blocks, roll blocks, leg blocks, lap blocks, knee blocks, and cartwheel blocks. Any block that keeps the tackler away from the man with the ball is an acceptable block. For the most part, however, young players should spend their time perfecting the basic shoulder and body blocks.

BASICS FOR BLOCKERS

1. Desire is most important. You must *want* to hit.
2. Block "through" the tackler.
3. Make contact; get under your opponent and then lift him off his feet.
4. Stay on your feet and maintain contact with your man.
5. If you block high, you will be whipped. Stay low and you do the whipping
6. Drive, hit, drive.

GET UNDER YOUR OPPONENT

TACKLING

Tackling is the art of using the hands, arms, or body to stop a ball carrier, and it is as basic a skill as blocking. As a player on defense, you do everything you can legally do to stop the other team from moving the ball toward your goal.

A chain is only as strong as the weakest link. A team's defense is only as strong as the tackling ability of each member. All players must know how to tackle, and tackling is a skill that must be learned.

Some coaches teach that the techniques for tackling are essentially the same as the techniques for shoulder and body blocks, except that in tackling one can use the hands and arms. There *are* certain skills acquired in practicing blocking that are carried over to tackling, but there are also different techniques involved. Most coaches agree, though, that tackling is 80 percent intensity and desire and 20 percent form.

Tackles may be made from the front, side, or rear of the man with the ball. It goes without saying that players with the ball do not willingly allow their opponents to meet them head-on. These are known as "straight shots," in the language of football players. But linebackers and deep defensive backs rushing toward the ball carrier, and linemen bursting past blockers at the line of scrimmage, do frequently get the chance to hit their men from the front.

To make this kind of tackle, keep your eyes open and directed at the ball carrier's midsection. Come at him with your feet wide apart and your weight under control. This means that you are in balance and ready to hurl your body at him, but also able to shift in any direction to meet his swerve.

Make contact with him with the full surface of your shoulder. Hit him low enough down

HEAD-ON TACKLE

from the waist so that you can wrap your arms
around his legs and lock them to stop him
from taking another step. Try not to grab him
too high up on his legs. If his knees are free
and he can keep them pumping up and down,
he may break your tackle.

Encircle both arms around the runner's
legs and pull them toward you, then drive
through with your shoulder. If you can lift
him off the ground slightly as you move him
back, he will not be able to add extra inches
to his run.

More often than not you won't be able to
get a straight shot at the runner. Under such
circumstances you shoot for the ball carrier's
knees, grab hold, and hang on. One hand
clutching an ankle may not fell the runner,
but may slow him down enough so that a teammate can reach him. Ball carriers have been
slowed and even stopped by tacklers holding
on only to a thigh pad or knee guard.

In general, tackles from one side or from
the rear are made as much like front tackles
as possible. That is, you make contact, wrap
your arms around his legs if you can, drag him
down to the ground however you can.

Practically all open-field tackles not made
from the rear by overtaking the ball carrier

are "angle tackles." This is not to say that angle tackles are not also made near the line of scrimmage, or in the line. An angle tackle is a tackle in which the tackler cuts the angle of space the ball carrier has to maneuver in, forcing him toward the side line. The runner is probably faster than the tackler or he would not be out in the open. Pinch the ball carrier toward the side line or force him toward your teammates who are pursuing him from the other side.

Remember that near the side line, the chalk mark is on your team. If you are after a man who is running near the side line, a push that knocks him out of bounds will stop his progress as well as a tackle. Keep the ball carrier between you and the side line, forcing him closer to the marker.

When you do make your dive, throw yourself well in front of the runner. Aim your

PUSH HIM OUT OF BOUNDS

OPEN-FIELD TACKLE

shoulder midway between the runner's knees and hips. Your head and shoulder should be across the runner's path and in front of him, both arms squeezing his knees.

Timing—driving for the ball carrier at the precisely right time—is all-important. Make your move too early and the runner will be able to sidestep you. Move too late and he can push off your tackle try with a straight-arm.

Keep in mind that as a tackler you are primarily concerned with stopping the ball carrier's advance in any legal way you can. It is not legal to tackle a ball carrier when he is out of bounds or after the ball has been whistled "dead" by an official. The rules do not allow a tackler to grasp an opponent's face protector. But "horse-collaring," which is

99

grabbing the runner around the neck or shoulders, or "clotheslining," in which the ball carrier runs into your extended arm and is stopped as though he had run into a stretched clothesline, are perfectly legal. Many coaches teach their players to use a high tackle, in which you clamp your arms around the ball carrier's arms to prevent a lateral pass.

The rules say that a ball carrier is down, his advance stopped, when any part of his body, except his hands or feet, touches the ground. Drag him down, wrestle him down, knock him out of bounds or off his feet with a block. Any legal move that stops the progress of the man with the ball toward your goal is a tackle.

BASICS FOR TACKLERS
1. Tackling depends on desire and intensity.
2. Aim to hit the ball carrier at a specific point.
3. Keep your eyes open, follow the ball. Ball carriers *do* fumble.
4. Keep on your feet and off your stomach.
5. Your target is through and beyond the ball carrier. Drive for it.
6. Drive, hit, drive.

7

The Center

Thus far we have talked about football in general and about playing the game as a team. Now let's turn to individual positions and to the special techniques of playing end, back, quarterback, kicker, and lineman. The logical place to start is with the *center*.

The position is well-named, for he is truly the center of almost every play. His main job is to put the ball in play, to hand back or snap back the football quickly to the quarterback, to the man who is holding the ball for field-goal tries, to the back who is going to carry the ball when the play calls for such a direct pass, or to the kicker in a punt situation.

You know that after the kickoff the team with the ball goes on offense, and the rules require that at least seven men be on the front line when a play starts. Left and right ends, left and right tackles, left and right guards, **101**

102 and the center make up the offensive line. The positions of the other linemen may vary in relation to the ball. That is, there is no set alignment they must take; the center *could* be on either end of the line with the other linemen all to one side, or there may be any number on either side of the center, as long as the total is at least seven. But the center is always over the ball.

Except for the center, though, an offensive lineman cannot play as far ahead of or behind the ball as he likes. As you know, the rulebook defines the line of scrimmage for each team as a vertical plane that runs through the point of the ball nearest the team's goal line. In other words, there are two lines of scrimmage, one for the offensive team and one for the defensive team. The space between them is called the neutral zone.

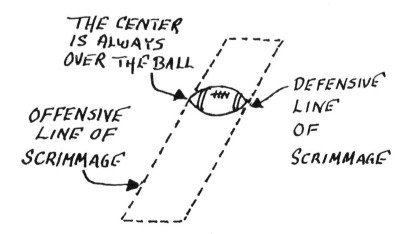

THE CENTER IS ALWAYS OVER THE BALL

OFFENSIVE LINE OF SCRIMMAGE

DEFENSIVE LINE OF SCRIMMAGE

A player on the offense is on his scrimmage line when he faces his opponent's goal with his shoulders about parallel to the line and with his head not more than 12 inches behind it. The defense can put as many or as few men on the line of scrimmage as they like at the start of play and they do not have to stand within 12 inches of it, but neither team can line up in or move into the neutral zone before the ball is snapped. If a player on the offense or defense crosses the line of scrimmage before the snap, he will be called offside and his team will be penalized 5 yards.

Many coaches will tell you that of all the players in the offensive line the center is the most important. Some say he is the most valuable man of the entire offensive unit, even more valuable than the quarterback. One coach we talked with about centers stated flatly that the center is *all*-important.

"Without a good dependable center," he said, "an offense cannot even get off the ground. You may have on your team a potential All-American back, a sweetheart of a passer, and a crew of fine receivers. They would all be helpless if your center could not get the ball to the ball carrier, kicker, or passer!"

As a center the basic skill you need is a sure hand in getting the ball to your quarterback— or to other backs when called upon to do so— at the right time. Most of the fumbles that occur when a quarterback is receiving the ball from center are the result of a poor snapback. Because the timing of the play depends on your snap, your delivery must be grooved so that the ball gets to the quarterback or other back at just the right time, *every* time. Timing and consistency come only with practice—and practice and practice.

Learning the proper stance and developing a good grip on the ball before the snapback are important to the center, but no inflexible rules can be laid down. Each center will have his own style. Of course, the stance and grip will vary depending on whether you are right- or left-handed and whether you are delivering the ball the short distance up into the waiting hands of your quarterback or making the longer direct pass back to a ball carrier, a punter, or the ball holder in kicking situations.

Centers also acquire, or have naturally, prejudices as to whether the lacing of the ball should face up, down, or off to one side. Referees prefer that you ask them to place the ball on the ground the way you want it rather than adjust it yourself after *they* have positioned it. You can tilt the ball before the snap, usually slanting it upward, but the officials will not allow you to move the ball before the snap in a way that will make the other team think you are actually beginning your delivery. They would be drawn offside unfairly. If you do move the ball before the actual snap, the official will call an offside penalty, all right, but against your team!

The center's stance differs from the three-point stance. Your feet are even and spread slightly wider than your shoulders, knees bent a little and turned in slightly. Your posterior should be a little higher than your shoulders, your head should be up, your eyes looking upward, neck relaxed, shoulders square, back straight. The ball rests on the ground in front of you, one pointed end facing you. Grasp it with your right hand—your left if you are left-handed—holding it like a passer, somewhat forward of the ball's middle.

THE CENTER'S STANCE

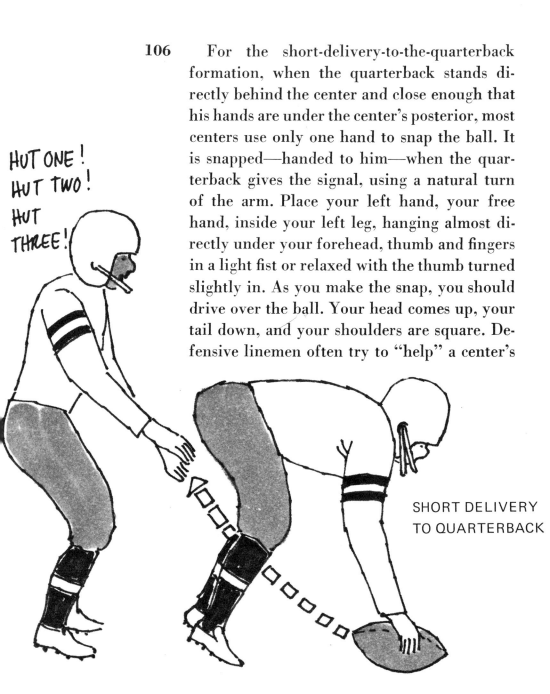

HUT ONE!
HUT TWO!
HUT
THREE!

For the short-delivery-to-the-quarterback formation, when the quarterback stands directly behind the center and close enough that his hands are under the center's posterior, most centers use only one hand to snap the ball. It is snapped—handed to him—when the quarterback gives the signal, using a natural turn of the arm. Place your left hand, your free hand, inside your left leg, hanging almost directly under your forehead, thumb and fingers in a light fist or relaxed with the thumb turned slightly in. As you make the snap, you should drive over the ball. Your head comes up, your tail down, and your shoulders are square. Defensive linemen often try to "help" a center's

SHORT DELIVERY
TO QUARTERBACK

drive by grabbing his helmet or shoulder guard and jerking him sprawling on his face. Keeping your free hand relaxed may save you a jammed finger or two in your instinctive reaction to break the stunt.

If you are a beginning center, you may want to use your free hand as a guide, gripping the ball anywhere you like, dropping it away from the ball as the oval slaps into the palm of the quarterback's hand. Snaps look easy because rarely do you see one fumbled in a game. But the apparent ease comes because center and quarterback have practiced snaps together so often that the rhythm and timing are grooved for both.

Quite naturally, beginning centers find it difficult to stop thinking of the hard charge they can expect from their opponent on the other side of the line of scrimmage after the snap, but this is apt to be disastrous. If you worry too much about it, you are likely to snap the ball poorly. Concentrating on making a good delivery of the ball must be your first concern.

For the longer, direct passbacks to ball carriers in the single-wing or double-wing formations, and when making a direct snap for a kicking play, things change for the center.

The stance is wider. You look under and through your legs, seeing your target upside down. You take a firmer grasp of the ball and use both hands. The right hand grips the front end of the ball and the left hand is under and around the back point of the oval. The main force of the passback comes from the right hand, the left hand acting as a guide. Your weight must be on your feet, and you put only a light pressure on the ball. A proper snap will spiral the ball to the receiver. This is much easier to handle than an end-over-end passback.

The spiral snapback differs from an end-over-end snap in that you twist your wrist as the ball leaves the ground. This gives it a spin that causes the oval to bore through the air in a spiraling motion like a drill. This twist often does not come naturally. You must practice until you automatically give the ball the right amount of spin.

For punts, you must snap the ball a rather long distance—usually 13 yards—and the passback must be accurate. The ball should arrive chest-high to the kicker, certainly no lower than waist-high. The snapback for a field-goal try or try-for-point kick after touchdown is around 7 yards. The ball should arrive in the ball holder's hands at a speed and height that will allow him to place it on the ground quickly and accurately for the kicker. This will vary and must be worked out between you and the holder.

Snapbacks to the ball carrier for running plays change depending on the type of play, on whether it is a sweep, slash off-tackle, cutback, reverse, straight buck. Sometimes you will have to snap the ball forcefully, throwing it a little in front of the runner as he takes a step in the direction of the play. This is called "leading the runner." Sometimes a higher, slower pass is called for.

109

But as center, you cannot concern yourself entirely with the snap. True, you must first concentrate your attention on it, but the instant after the snap is made you become a blocker in the offensive line.

You get your head up, elbows out, and you make your charge. Teammates on either side of you should tip you off when a defensive player shifts position on you after you lower your head to make direct snapbacks. If your opponent has moved to one side of you, you are apt to hit nothing but air when you charge forward!

You draw a bead on the defensive man you have been assigned to block. Your coach will of course decide on your blocking assignment and the kind of block you make for the various types of play. For a power sweep, a power drive, a trap play, you usually double-team block with your guard against the defensive guard, right or left depending on the direction of the play. You would use a shoulder block. On quick slant plays you may be assigned to block a linebacker or cornerback. You use whatever type of block that will be effective for the downfield situation.

On pass plays the center becomes a vital man, helping to form the protective pocket for the passer. You use the short, jabbing blocks of the pass protector. In kicking situations, the center is a part of the holding wall that keeps defensive men from getting through the line and ruining the kick. You use the stationary block.

As center you spearhead the offense. You are the leading force. You must be careful to hold to a regular rhythm when you hand back the ball. Otherwise your teammates may "jump the ball"—start their forward charges before your snap. This will cost your team a 5-yard penalty for being offside. Good centers are truly the center of play.

BASICS FOR CENTERS

1. Concentrate on making the snap first.
2. Keep your head up and use your eyes when you snap the ball to the quarterback.
3. Accuracy and consistency in passbacks are all-important.
4. As a blocker, outplay your opponent from the first play. Gain the psychological advantage by taking charge.
5. Practice snaps to your quarterback. Practice snapbacks to punters and to holders for place kicks.

8
Offensive and Defensive Line Play

OFFENSIVE LINE PLAY

In addition to the center, the offensive line contains guards and tackles. They are often called interior linemen to distinguish them from the ends, who are part of the seven men required on the line of scrimmage but who are not really linemen.

There are, of course, variations in the play of guards and tackles. For example, each is assigned a different opponent to block in different game situations. But the basic job of a guard or tackle is the same: to move his opponent away from the path of the ball carrier.

Guards and tackles are strictly linemen. They very rarely get a chance to carry the ball. A guard or tackle *could* be made eligible to catch a forward pass if he was put at the end of the line of scrimmage before the start of a play, but this is rarely done. Once in a while a guard

or tackle intercepts a pass or recovers a fum-
ble and takes the ball into the end zone. But such touchdowns are unusual.

To play guard or tackle well, you must be intelligent, aggressive, and courageous. You must develop to a high degree whatever nature has provided you in the way of quick reactions, speed afoot, and strength.

"Guards are fullbacks with their brains beat out!" This supposedly funny remark might have been appropriate in the early days of football when the chief job of a guard was to act as part of the "beef trust," running ahead of the ball carrier to shove the defense a few yards toward the ball carrier's goal. Listen to a pro guard or college guard, or even one playing for a well-coached high school, talk about his position today and you will understand how ridiculous the old joke is.

"Keeping pressure on the defensive tackle," "folding on the linebacker," "handling the player who comes at you all-out hard, and the ones who hold up to 'read' you and then react," "pulling out to run interference for the ball carrier" are expressions modern guards use to describe some of their functions. Nor do tackles like to be thought of as having "strong backs and weak minds"!

The first thing an interior lineman—guard or tackle—must do is settle on his stance and use that same stance always, whenever he lines up at scrimmage. If, in blocking your opponent to the right, you used a different stance from the one you took when you were planning to block him to the left, he would soon be able to "read" you. He would predict your move before the ball was snapped and it would be easy for him to deal with your block.

He would have a big edge if you used a special stance when you were going to pass block. When a defensive man *knows* the next play will be a pass, instead of a run, he doesn't have to worry about a ball carrier. He can concentrate on getting by you to try to ruin the quarterback's throw.

Of course, every lineman need not take exactly the same stance. Boys differ in height, weight, and in the length of their arms and legs. Some are right-handed and some are left-handed. The main thing to keep in mind is that you must fix on a stance that is comfortable for you, one that allows you to move smoothly forward, backward, or to either side—and never vary this stance.

As a beginning lineman, you will most likely be playing against opponents who have little or no more experience than you. You **115** will probably not have to contend with an opponent who "holds you up to read you and then reacts." But sooner or later you will meet this wily kind of player, who does not charge hard at you when the ball is snapped, but waits for you to commit yourself to the action you plan to take. You can see that once he knows what your move will be, in what direction you are heading, he can make his own move and defeat yours more easily. So learn from the start to mask your intentions until the last possible instant.

"HE'S TAKING THE END RUN STANCE"

Whether you are a young or more experienced player, your coach will expect you to block well. On running plays that call for a ball carrier to smash through the middle of the line, offensive guards and tackles must be able to charge the man they are assigned to block and move him out of the ball carrier's path. If the striking point of a running play is "off-tackle," this means that the ball carrier will be heading for a spot in the line between the tackle and the end. The offensive guards and tackles must move the men they are assigned to block *in,* toward the center of the field, and out of the way of the ball carrier.

On wide running plays such as sweeps and reverses, guards almost always "pull out" of the line when the ball carrier is going to run around their side of the line. They lead the interference, helping to clear defensive ends, linebackers, or defensive backs from the ball carrier's path. Sometimes tackles pull out, too, so both jobs require knowledge of the techniques of pulling.

Instead of driving across the neutral zone at your opponent as you do when the ball carrier is going through the middle of the line, you swing back away from the line of scrimmage and run parallel to it. You must get out

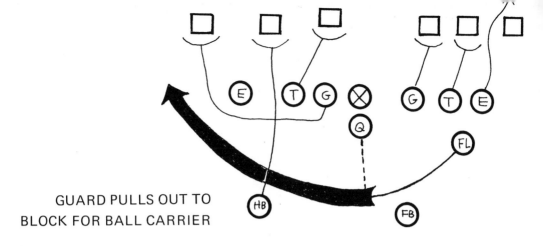

GUARD PULLS OUT TO
BLOCK FOR BALL CARRIER

quickly or you will gum up the play by clog-
ging the ball carrier's path. Pulling from the
line is not a natural movement and most time
is lost in getting started. A lot of practice is
needed to perfect the moves and learn proper
timing.

Suppose the play is a sweep, in which a running back takes a short pass from the quarterback—a pitchout—and heads for the side line.
If he is to "turn the corner," get around the
end of the line and start his run downfield, the
defensive end and defensive back on that side
must be blocked out of the way before the ball
carrier gets there. Say you are a little slow in
pulling out of the line and as a result do not
get out there in time to put a block on the defensive end. He gives you a hard shove—into
your ball carrier. The ball carrier has not even
crossed the line of scrimmage, and the play
loses yardage!

117

GUARD PULLING OUT FROM LINE

In order to pull out fast and sure, at the snap of the ball you pivot your body. Move the foot on the side toward which you are going to run diagonally backward and point it in the direction of your run. With your other foot take a second step, also diagonally backward. The initial drive comes from this foot and leg. Push off and take a third step, with your foot now parallel to the line of scrimmage. Start your normal stride, but do not straighten your body as you complete the pivot. You are still running low. If you do not pivot your body and step and drive off the second foot properly, you won't get out fast enough to help. And you may, just as we have seen, ruin the play.

The best weapon an offensive lineman has for blocking on running plays is the shoulder block. Remember—it cannot be emphasized too strongly—that you do not lunge at your man when you throw this block. Uncoil and move into him with your feet under your body and your weight under control. Make contact with your shoulder, side of your neck, and upper arm. Keep in contact and move your man backward or in whatever direction the play calls for by bracing your feet and driving in short, piston-like digging steps. Keep your head up and focus your eyes beyond and through your target.

BRACE YOUR
FEET AND DRIVE

FORM A POCKET TO PROTECT THE PASSER

In today's football the offensive line must be able to protect their passer by keeping the defensive men "off the quarterback's back." Most coaches want their blockers to form a pocket, and as we have seen, pass blocking is different from other kinds of blocking.

Your stance is the same as you line up, but you do not charge across the neutral zone at an opponent. You get up from your stance into a semi-crouch, your arms in blocking position— close to the chest, elbows out wide. You make contact with your opponent. Guards block the defensive tackles and offensive tackles block defensive ends.

The block is basically a shoulder block, but you can use any legal move you know to keep your opponent off-balance. You hit your opponent, bounce him off-balance, and make sure he stays off-balance by keeping pressure on him, hitting and hitting again and again. You must stay in balance yourself and keep your hands away from him. Remember that you cannot hold him.

Pass blocking is a must for a passing attack to work, and a good passing attack is very important in winning games. Suppose your team is behind on the scoreboard. There is not much time to play and the ball is a long way from the opponents' goal. Your quarterback calls a bomb, a long pass play. The receivers must have time to get downfield and in position to catch the ball. The quarterback needs time to locate a receiver who is in the open and make the pass. You and your mates on the offensive line must give them the necessary time by keeping charging defense men away from the quarterback.

You hit them and bounce them and keep them from getting to the quarterback, and a receiver works open and is spotted by the passer. The pass is completed for a winning touchdown. The receiver and the quarterback will get the headlines, but you and your fellow blockers know that the touchdown is as much yours as the receiver's and passer's.

Coaches like to use their strongest and roughest linemen as their tackles. Most often a team's bread-and-butter plays—the plays they depend on for a sure gain—are run "off-tackle" or "inside the tackle." Ball carriers run between guard and tackle (on either side of the line, of course) on inside-tackle plays. As we have seen, they slant between tackle and end on off-tackle plays. If the offensive tackle cannot block his man out of the way, cannot open a hole in the defensive line for the ball carrier, there won't be much yardage gained.

Good tackles must *like* close, rough action. Often the tackle must hold his block longer than a guard or center. He is frequently assigned to block the defensive man who is most dangerous to the passer, the rusher who has proved by ingenuity, strength, or what have you that he is the man most difficult to block out and keep blocked out.

As a guard, your assignment most of the time will be the defensive guard or tackle on your side of the line, depending on what formation the defense is using. Almost always you **123** will be expected to check block or brush block the defensive guard or tackle and go on to block a linebacker or defensive back. This means that you knock the guard or tackle off-balance and hold the block only long enough to keep him from charging across the line of scrimmage. Then you brush past him to throw another block at the linebacker to keep him out of the way of your ball carrier. You already

KNOCK THE DEFENSIVE GUARD
OR DEFENSIVE TACKLE OFF BALANCE.

THEN MOVE ON
TO THROW BLOCK
ON THE LINEBACKER.

124 know that as a guard you must learn to lead the interference for the ball carrier on wide running plays.

Agility, speed, alertness, intelligence, and aggressiveness are the marks of all offensive linemen. The coach of a southern football team once put in capsule form what he looked for in guards and tackles.

"I want them to be a-jile, mo-bile, and hostile," he said, emphasizing the first syllable in each word. Such a player is sure to be welcomed by any coach.

BASICS FOR OFFENSIVE LINEMEN

1. Always line up in the same stance.
2. Your blocking assignment is important to the success of the play. Carry out your assignment.
3. Keep alert.
4. Maintain contact with the opponent you are blocking.
5. A lineman pulling from the line to run interference will interfere with the play more than help his teammates unless he moves out *quickly*.
6. Get the jump on the defense and keep them off-balance.

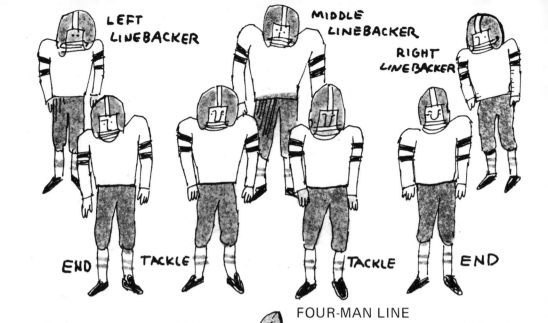

LEFT LINEBACKER

MIDDLE LINEBACKER

RIGHT LINEBACKER

END TACKLE TACKLE END

FOUR-MAN LINE

DEFENSIVE LINE PLAY

No matter what their position, the chief aim of all defensive linemen is the same: get at the ball carrier, passer, or kicker.

As we have seen, in the 4-3 defensive set, the center and the two guards are dropped from the front wall, leaving two defensive ends and two defensive tackles. They try to evade blockers and get to the ball carrier on running plays. They rush the passer on pass plays, trying to get to him before he can throw or to hurry him into making a bad pass.

Immediately behind the front four are the right, middle, and left linebackers. They are the men who on running plays most often

125

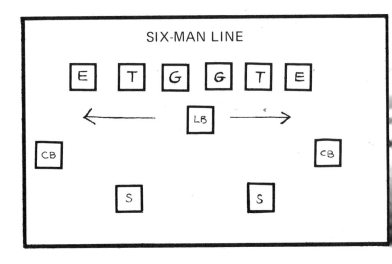

SIX-MAN LINE

tackle the ball carrier just as he pops through a hole in the line. On pass plays they also cover the short receivers. These are the men who run last beyond the line of scrimmage to catch passes instead of far down the field. The linebackers cover offensive players coming out of the backfield to become receivers—the halfbacks and fullbacks.

Any defensive set with fewer than seven men in the front line will have linebackers. A six-man line allows the center to roam from end to end behind the front wall, adding defensive strength at the point of attack. A defense with five men up front—a five-man line **126** —will have three linebackers playing immedi-

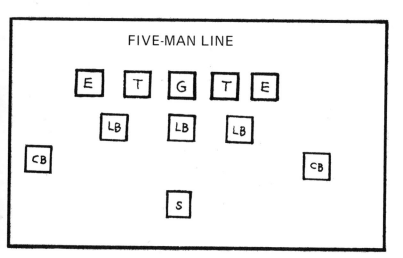

FIVE-MAN LINE

E T G T E

LB LB LB

CB   CB

S

ately behind the line to plug holes. Linebackers make most of the tackles on running plays that go through the line, and they also help in turning back sweeps, reverses, and end-around plays.

Linebackers also join the linemen in the pass rush when there is a "red dog" or "blitz." As we have seen, these terms mean an all-out rush at the passer, which takes place when the defensive captain believes the play coming up will be a pass. The aim is to overwhelm the offensive blockers and smear the passer.

A driving charge, a "nose for following the ball," and sure tackling are the basics for good defensive line play.

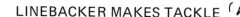

LINEBACKER MAKES TACKLE

9
Offensive and Defensive Backs

OFFENSIVE BACKS

Usually the fellow who carries the ball for long gains and touchdowns gets the applause of the fans. *You* know that the star pass receiver or the man who runs through the defensive line with the ball would be nowhere without solid blocking to spring him free of tacklers. The average spectator, though, sees only the ball carrier. Almost every boy dreams of carrying the ball and his team to glorious victories. Perhaps you want to be a runner, too—a halfback or a fullback.

Are you fast enough to move from your position behind the quarterback, take his "pitchout" to you, and "turn the corner" —get around the end of the line on sweeps? Do you have the drive and strength to break through the defensive line, the quickness to slice through a slit of daylight before the hole

OFFENSIVE BACK

in the line closes? Can you go out for a pass
and grab the ball as if your hands were
smeared with a magic glue? Can you block a
charging defensive man who is roaring in to
tackle another ball carrier?

If you can answer "Yes" to all of the above
questions, you are on your way to becoming
an all-American back. If you can answer, "I
am reasonably fast and strong, and I can learn
to block and catch passes," your coach will
welcome you as a candidate for a running back
job.

In the past, halfbacks always carried the ball
on such running plays as sweeps, reverses, off-
tackle slants, and any others in which speed
and deceptiveness were important. Halfbacks
were lighter in weight in the old days and thus
likely to be faster, more capable of speeding
down the open field for the long gainer, or
going out for medium and long passes.

129

The fullback was the power man, the one who would "bull" into the defensive line and pick up short yardage, the yard or two needed for the first down. He was heavier, slower, but more powerful and rugged than the halfbacks. Part of his job was to block for the fleeter half-backs; he had to be an exceptional blocker.

But no longer are the differences between fullbacks and halfbacks as great. The fact is that on today's teams the men who carry the football are often lumped together under the name "running back," and they all have the same duties. The halfback must be powerful enough to ram through the defensive line and fast enough to run sweeps. The fullback must be speedy enough to run his share of sweeps and reverses while still being the short-yardage power man.

One of the first things a back must learn is the proper stance. Your coach will decide whether you should assume the three-point stance already described in Chapter Six, or the upright stance with your hands on knees. Some coaches favor a wider stance for the fullback than for halfbacks; but by and large, backs assume similar positions before the snap.

In the upright stance your feet are on a line parallel to the line of scrimmage and spread

UPRIGHT STANCE

apart comfortably, about 18 inches. The key word here is "comfortably." Your arms should be straight, with your hands on your knees. Your knees are bent a little. Your weight should be on the balls of your feet, although you may want to shift your weight a little to one side or the other, depending on the direction you are planning to go to carry out a particular assignment. Be careful not to vary your stance too much, though. If you do, a defensive man who is keying on you—watching your movements closely—will be able to read the play before the ball is even snapped.

Whatever stance you use, keep in mind two important rules. Take the same stance on every play, and if you are to receive the ball from either the center or the quarterback, keep your eyes focused on the ball until the center snaps it. Without realizing it, young, inexperienced players sometimes tip their opponents off to the next play, virtually telling them it will be a pass, a running play through the line, or a sweep, by a change in stance or by some other little mannerism. Such giveaways are fatal to your offense.

Do not concentrate so hard on the man you expect to block that you stare at him. Do not wet your fingers when you are going to receive a pass. Do not glance toward the spot at the

DON'T GIVE
AWAY THE
NEXT PLAY

line of scrimmage where you plan to run.
Wipe your hands on your jersey, hitch up your
pants, make any small move—and an alert opponent will spot you as the ball carrier and be
ready for you.

Knowledgeable football people say that "all
backs look alike behind their own line of scrimmage." This means that all backs are helpless
if tacklers get to them before they can reach
the line of scrimmage. A ball carrier shows his
skill at and beyond the line. Good blocking or
a trick play that catches the defense off guard
will get the ball carrier past the line of scrimmage. But from there on the success of the play
will depend on his ability to run with the ball.

Start your run with short steps, your legs
pumping, your knees high. Learn to "cut," to
change direction sharply. You must be able to
switch instinctively from a lateral course on
the field, in which you are running nearly parallel to the line of scrimmage, to a forward
course. And you must make your cut at the
precise moment a hole opens in the defensive
line. Your effectiveness as a running back will
be based to a very large extent on this ability.

Run hard, at top speed, with your head up
and your eyes open and carry your weight a
little forward. Linemen love a fast running

MAKE YOUR CUT THE MOMENT
THE HOLE OPENS IN DEFENSIVE LINE.

THEN GO . . . .

TOUCHDOWN!

back because then they do not have to hold
their blocks for a long time. The good runner drives hard through the hole they have
opened up for him before their opponents can
recover from the block.

When you are about to be tackled, lower
your shoulders and fight for that extra yard,
even inches. How often have you seen the referee call for the chains to be brought in from
the side lines to measure the yardage for a
first down, then indicate that the ball is short
"this much"—a few inches? If each back gives
just a little more, battles for an extra inch or
two each time he carries the ball, the extra
inches may add up to a first down. Your team
will not be forced to give up possession of the
134 ball.

PROTECT THAT FOOTBALL!

Be sure to protect the ball, too, when you are tackled. Put both hands around it, and pull your arms, the ball, and your legs in close to your body. Tuck your chin in to your chest and relax. In this position you will be less likely to be injured and much less likely to have the ball knocked loose for a fumble.

As a runner you must also be able to judge distances accurately. You must always know how far you are from the side line, how far away are the tacklers coming at you. You must know how to use your blockers, how to help them help you to gain yardage. The ability to straight-arm and to carry the ball properly are skills the running back also needs.

The straight-arm or stiff-arm is valuable in getting past a tackler. Relax your arm and bend

135

136 your elbow slightly to bring your forearm almost parallel with the ground. An instant before the tackler comes in range and is about to try to ground you, lock your wrist, elbow, and shoulder and hit him with the heel of your hand. The push combined with the tackler's own momentum steers him away from you.

It is important to be able to straight-arm with either arm, and you must learn to shift the ball from one hand to the other when the tackler approaches from the side on which you are carrying it. Here comes the danger of fumbling. Few things are more frustrating to your teammates than to block perfectly and spring

STRAIGHT-ARM OR STIFF-ARM

a runner loose—only to watch it all go down the drain because he fumbles the ball!

Some backs carry the ball recklessly out in the open in one hand. They may look very flashy—until they are hit by a hard tackle and the ball is knocked free. It could happen to you!

Sometimes sheepish-looking boys are seen on college campuses and in high school halls carrying footballs wherever they go. Ask one why he does so, and he will probably tell you:

"I fumbled a couple of times in a game. Coach is making me lug this football around, giving me the cure."

"How can that help cure you of fumbling?" you ask.

"Well, Coach said maybe I'd get the idea that a football is something to treasure and hang on to when you get it in a game, not something to be handled like a bag of trash. Every time you pick the thing up to go to your next class, you think about coaches screaming at you to hang on to the ball!"

The rules allow the defense to "tackle the ball." If they can jar it loose, make you fumble it, tearing it from your grasp, it is a free ball. Anyone can recover it. See to it that you don't handle the ball "like a bag of trash" but treas-

OH! OH!

DON'T CARRY BALL LIKE A BAG OF TRASH!

ure it and hang on to it. Unless you have a huge hand, it is best not to carry the football grasped in your hand alone. Tuck the oval against your body, using hand, forearm, and body to keep it firm.

Any list of football greats would include John W. Heisman, who coached teams at Oberlin, Akron, Auburn, Clemson, Georgia Tech, Pennsylvania, Washington, and Jefferson and Rice during thirty-six years of active coaching. The famed Heisman Trophy, awarded each year to an outstanding college football player, the top player of the year, is named after Coach Heisman. He was fond of telling his pupils, "This is a football—an elliptical sphere, or prolate spheroid, wrapped in a leathern casing. . . . Better you should die as a small boy than fumble it!"

All ball carriers must learn moves to help them evade tacklers. They must know how to

FUMBLE!

change pace, sidestep, cross-step, veer, and pivot. It would be a rare animal that could teach you to straight-arm or carry a football well, but by playing with a pet dog, or even a cat, you can improve tremendously your footwork in the open field.

Try to catch your pet. Watch how it increases and decreases its speed, how it whirls or pivots, how it sidesteps to get away from you. In trying to keep up with it, you will develop skills of movement that nature has given to many animals, humans included.

To change pace, drift along at a controlled speed, then shift into high gear with a burst of speed that leaves the tackler "hitting nothing but atmosphere."

To sidestep your opponent, shift your weight to the toe of the leg nearest the tackler. Your knee should be bent and your body leaning forward. When the tackler lunges at you, hit with a straight-arm and leap to the side, away from him.

139

CROSS-STEP

The cross-step is similar to a sidestep but you run directly at the tackler, and as he makes his move, you cross one leg in front of the other and spring off in another direction. Perfect this maneuver and you may read about yourself in the newspaper as "swivel hips" and "ball-bearing hips" and "loose hips."

Veering is a sharp change of direction executed quickly. You lead in one direction with one leg, then take a short step to the side with the other to slant your body the opposite way.

Pivoting is similar to veering except that the tackler is used as the pivotal point. You plant the foot on the side from which the tackler is coming firmly on the ground, hit the side of his helmet with your hand, and use him as a base to spin away. You should use short steps and high knee action and maintain contact with the ground in this dodge. You

140

PIVOTING

invite injury if you leap into the air in executing a pivot.

As a back you must also perfect your pass-receiving ability. Pass patterns for backs are usually not long routes compared to those run by the wideouts, the split ends, and flankerbacks. Because of his position on the field behind the quarterback, a running back takes too much time to "go long" for a pass. Notice that in the diagram of patterns, backs receive most of the passes thrown to them either behind the line of scrimmage or just beyond it. Flare patterns or safety valves, cutouts, screens, look-ins—these are the routes running backs take.

Another pattern for backs is the screen pass. The guard and tackle on the side of the field to which the ball is to be thrown first block the defensive tackle and the defensive end. Then **141**

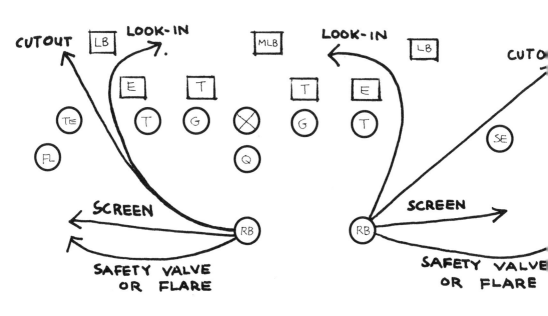

PASS PATTERNS OF BACKS

they pull back from the line of scrimmage to form with the tight end and the flanker a "screen" of blockers. The quarterback flips a short pass to a running back who is behind the screen. Keep in mind that the tight end may change position with the split end and stand on either end of the offensive line. So a screen pass may be aimed at either the right or left side of the line.

Finally, never forget that as a running back you must master thoroughly the techniques of blocking. When the other running back carries the ball instead of you, blocking for him is an important part of your job.

BASICS FOR RUNNING BACKS

1. Carry the ball so it cannot be dislodged easily from your grasp.
2. Develop your ability to cut.
3. Use your blockers.
4. Practice maneuvers that will help you to avoid tacklers.
5. Drive for those extra inches. Make that "second effort" which may break you loose from the grasp of tacklers and enable you to go for more yardage.

In today's terminology defensive halfbacks are more often called cornerbacks or cornermen. Safeties are also defensive backs. They are the deep defenders who play behind the halfbacks.

In the past the defensive halfbacks would have been known as "left" and "right" halfbacks, but today these terms are no longer popular either. Instead, football people speak of the "strong" and "weak" sides of the field. The strong side of the offensive formation is so-called because normally the tight end and flankerback are positioned on that side. The cornerback who plays on this side of the field is known as the strong-side—or strong—cornerback. The weak side of the offensive formation is so-called because there is one less player on this side of the line. Usually the split end is positioned on the weak side. The cornerback playing on this side of the field is the weak-side—or weak—cornerback. Safeties too are known as strong and weak instead of left and right.

Cornerbacks are positioned 5 yards behind the line of scrimmage, although the number of yards is flexible. They are primarily protectors against passes, but they also play important parts in defending against sweeps, reverses, and end-arounds of the opponent's running game. Cornerbacks need to be sure tacklers.

But as a cornerback your first and foremost job is to defend against the passing game. In man-to-man coverage cornerbacks are assigned to cover the fastest and most dangerous receivers. With speed, deception, and quick reactions, you must match the moves of the receiver. You must be able to go to either side and backward as well as you run forward.

One of your jobs is to delay the potential receiver at the line of scrimmage. You must try

THE DEFENSIVE BACKS ARE THE SAFETIES AND CORNERBACKS

to stop him from getting away fast after the ball is snapped. A delaying tactic cornerbacks are using more and more at the line is the *bump-and-run*. This is not a new technique. As long as there have been pass receivers, defensive men have used similar moves.

Until the ball leaves the passer's hands, defenders look upon potential receivers as potential blockers too. The upcoming play can as well be a running play as a pass. If it is a run, the receiver will try to block you out of the way to make room for the ball carrier. So defenders have always bumped receivers, harassed them, kept them off-balance in whatever way possible to keep the offensive man from gaining an advantage—without holding him of course. The modern bump-and-run differs from an outright block in that the bumper sees to it that he is able to stick with the receiver after bumping him.

For example, suppose you are the strong-side cornerback assigned to cover the flanker-back. You bump him as the ball is snapped instead of waiting for him to move downfield. You try to knock him off-stride, then you run along with him, challenging him all the way. The bump-and-run is effective in man-to-man

STICK WITH THAT SPLIT END
LIKE MUSTARD PLASTER

coverage in which each defensive back covers a specified receiver.

If you are playing weak-side cornerback you are responsible for covering the split end. You stick with him like a mustard plaster.

As the strong-side safety you usually go out to cover the tight end on pass routes. The weak-side safety is often called the *free safety*. His assignment changes from play to play, depending on what the offense is doing. He is first responsible for keeping an eye on the running backs. When either back moves past the scrimmage line into a downfield pattern, the weak safety picks him up. If no back is running a pattern downfield, the safety is free to help out his teammates in covering the receiver

147

148 who is considered most dangerous. Almost always the tricky offensive receiver noted for outfooting the defensive player assigned to him in a one-on-one situation will be double-covered. This means two men try to prevent him from receiving a pass, and the free safety is most frequently the second defender.

Of course both safeties go after any ball carrier who gets past the cornerbacks.

As a defensive back responsible for covering pass receivers, you must keep in mind that they are smart. They will vary their routes, vary their moves. They will throw head fakes at you, aiming the head one way but moving in the opposite direction. They will throw body fakes. They will fake you with their eyes. You must develop your reflexes to combat these fakes.

There are just no cut-and-dried rules to follow in defending against a good receiver. One thing a defensive back can do is focus on the receiver's belt buckle. This will make you less vulnerable to head and shoulder fakes. Top receivers do not use techniques that fall into neat categories. A defensive back must stay loose, be ready to adjust and adapt to the receiver's moves.

DON'T BROOD OVER AN ERROR!

There will be times when you will get "burned." This means that a receiver will outsmart you and get in the clear, take the ball and go for a long gain, perhaps a touchdown. But you must stay aggressive, believe that a ball in the air is as much yours as the receiver's. Sometimes you will make mistakes, but such occasions must be shrugged off. It's not that you don't care. You learn from mistakes and you apply what you learn in future encounters with tricky receivers. But you must not brood over an error.

149

1. Work hard to develop skills to move to either side, or backward, in a running motion, while maintaining good balance.

2. Know pass patterns, study them. Know that certain patterns may be run from certain formations and in certain situations in the game.

3. Know how to catch the ball and practice the techniques. With your eyes on the ball, pluck it out of the air with relaxed fingers. Protect the football when you make an interception.

4. Develop your ability to control the receiver. Try to force him off his stride.

5. Deep backs especially must never allow a receiver to get behind them.

6. Call back and forth to other defensive backs and warn your mates of potential receivers in their area of the field. You must work together closely to cover opponents.

7. Practice against the better receivers on your own team. Never miss an opportunity to study future opponents in filmed or actual live game action.

10
End Play and Pass Receiving

END PLAY

As we have seen, the players at the extremities of the offensive line were known originally as *left end* and *right end*. They are still so named in such formations as the straight T, the single-wing, the double-wing, and punt formations in which the ends are not "split away" from their tackles. In the pro-set, though—in any formation where one end lines up several yards away from his tackle—the players at the extremities of the offensive line are known as tight end and split end.

You know, too, that an offense that uses two instead of three set backs—running backs—positions a fourth man in the backfield outside the tight end, toward the side line, and at least a yard behind the line of scrimmage. He is called a flanker—the flankerback.

The rule book states that the eligible pass receivers are: each player of the team on of-

fense who, at the snap, was on an end of the
scrimmage line (a total of two) and each
player who at the snap was at least one yard
behind the scrimmage line (a possible total
of four). Thus the split end, tight end, flanker,
and the running backs can all receive passes.

Split ends and flankers are primarily the
wideouts, the *long receivers*. They take the
deep passes, the long, dramatic "bombs"
thrown wide toward the side lines. They function primarily as pass receivers, although they
do block on occasion.

The tight end is expected to block, receive
passes, and even carry the ball in running
plays.

As a blocker, the tight end sometimes teams up with his tackle to block the defensive end and sometimes draws the assignment of blocking the end all by himself. Often he is called on to block the linebacker on his side of the field or to slant in and cut down the middle linebacker.

As a pass receiver the tight end runs a variety of pass routes—a slant-in pattern, a slant-out pattern, hook-in, hook-out, etc. These are mostly short routes which may take him 2 to 5 yards beyond the line of scrimmage. But a coach may come up with plays in which the tight end, or even a back, runs deep patterns to catch the defense off guard. A diagram later in this chapter shows a few pass routes run by tight ends—and by other receivers. Keep in mind that *any* receiver may run *any* pattern. And that all receivers, be they tight ends, split ends, or backs, learn a number of pass patterns. These are routes which are worked out in practice sessions. Without such prearranged patterns, the quarterback would not know where to expect to find his receivers on the field. Of course, the receiver may have to abandon his set route at times because a defensive back blocks it.

PASS PATTERNS OF ENDS

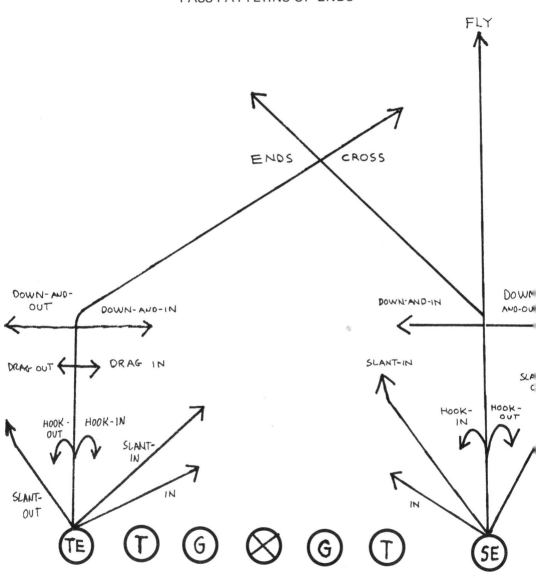

Sometimes the tight end becomes a ball carrier. In an end-around play, for example, he
moves from his position and sweeps across the
backfield toward the opposite end of the line
of scrimmage, taking either a hand-off or a
pitchout from the quarterback and carrying
the ball on around the flank.

Split ends and tight ends may position themselves on the right or left side of the line according to the play. When the tight end plays
tight to the left tackle, the formation is called
"strong left" or "left." When the tight end is
positioned near the right tackle the formation
is designated "strong right" or simply "right."
This shift of positioning between split end and
tight end is called "flip-flopping." The maneuver is designed to confuse the defense,
throwing blocking assignments out of line
long enough to give a small advantage to the
offense.

TIGHT END CARRIES BALL
IN END-AROUND PLAY

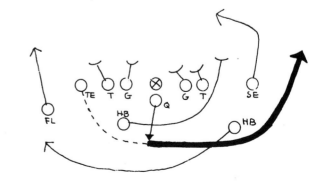

Rarely is the tight end positioned in the flanker spot, but there is no rule against it. A formation with the tight end playing a yard deep off the line is called an "inside formation."

The writer asked a coach what he would look for in the ideal tight end.

"Well, he would be something, I'll tell you! He would have height, good hands, better-than-fair weight, strength, and ruggedness to block. For carrying the ball on running plays and after catching passes, he would have the open-field elusiveness and leg drive of a running back. Add to these qualities desire, mobility, balance, guts, and stamina and you'd have a tight end who could do it all."

Unlike the tight end, the split end is not expected to block much, but he must know the techniques of blocking. Suppose a teammate has taken a pass. Perhaps he has run a shorter pass pattern than you, and you are between him and the goal line. One or both of the defensive safeties will be coming hard after him. The split end who knows how to block can "wash out" at least one threat to the man with the ball by throwing an effective block.

Whether you play tight end or split end, you

must keep in mind that different coaches make **157** different blocking assignments. You may be required to *pinch-block* when you work with your tackle to double-team a defensive end or tackle. This means that you crowd him toward your tackle's block. You will also drive shoulder blocks against linebackers and throw body blocks at defensive men downfield. You must know the techniques of different blocks and be able to execute them.

In offensive formations in which neither end is split away from the tackles, the jobs of the two ends change somewhat. The players still line up at the extremities of the line, but *both* ends will have blocking duties on running plays.

BASICS FOR ENDS

1. Ends are pass receivers. You must perfect the skills needed to run pass routes and catch the ball.
2. Ends are also called upon to block. You must work on different kinds of blocks.
3. Ends do sometimes carry the ball. You must develop running, feinting, and faking skills.

PASS RECEIVING

To be a top grabber of passes—tight end, split end, flanker, or back—there are certain skills you must acquire, certain things you must know. But there is one thing you must *not* know—fear. You can be sure that often you are going to be hit hard by a defensive man very soon after you catch the pass. But you must never take your eyes off the ball to assess the danger. In the language of football players, if you "hear footsteps" (feel or even see from the corner of your eye that an opponent is coming) you are "dead" (about as sure not to catch the ball as you would be if you ran away from it).

As a pass receiver you must become a "sticky fingers." You may be able to run dazzling pass patterns, to fake defenders "out of their shoes" and get out in the open and be ready to catch the ball. But these skills mean nothing if you cannot catch and hang on to the ball. Catch the ball in both hands, not against your chest. If your fingers are relaxed, you will **158** be much less likely to fumble the pass.

Keep your eyes on the ball. Never take as much as a peek at the field. Concentrate on "looking the ball into your hands." Top receivers concentrate to such degree that they are not even aware of a defender who may be within a foot or two of them. Every pass thrown to you belongs to you. Make every effort to catch and hang on to the ball.

Your hands should make a relaxed basket when catching a pass. "Giving with the pass" —going along naturally with the path of the ball once it hits your hands—will help you to handle a hard pass. Don't fight the ball, and be careful not to jab at it.

You must know as you run downfield in what direction the ball is heading, whether it is coming on your right or left side or in front of you. You may have to catch the ball over your shoulder in full stride, and you need to know which shoulder. Sometimes a passer will underthrow the ball, or it will be tipped and partly deflected by a charging defensive man.

YOUR HANDS MAKE
A RELAXED BASKET

BUTTONHOOK BACK WHEN PASS IS SHORT

160 You must be able to "fishhook" or "button-hook" back upfield and snag the ball when you judge that the pass is short.

Hardly ever is a pass receiver alone in the area where he expects to receive the pass. A defensive man, your cover, is usually only a few feet away, ready to prevent you from receiving, or to try to intercept the pass. You must be able to "grab the ball in heavy traffic." You know that the defensive man has a right to play the ball, and if he can grab it before you can, his team gains possession. So, if you cannot possibly catch the pass and your cover can, you make every effort to prevent him from intercepting and running the ball back toward your goal.

Getting open, which means maneuvering so you are not covered by a defensive man, is

THE DEFENSE WILL TRY TO HOLD YOU UP AT SCRIMMAGE

AND YOUR DEFENDER WILL TRY
TO INTERCEPT THE PASS

all-important for the receiver. Remember that the defense does everything it can to prevent receivers from getting open. First they try to hold up the receiver at the line of scrimmage. They try to stop him from getting away fast from the line once the ball has been snapped. This does *not* mean that they actually hold on to his body or his uniform—which is a foul —but they can use their hands to push and generally harass and slow down the receiver. You must use every means you know to avoid this delay.

Once the receiver is in the open field, defensive backs "pick him up" to try to prevent him from catching a pass thrown his way. They also try to be near enough to go after the ball when it is passed. A defender must not touch the receiver to hinder his progress once the ball leaves the passer's hands. This would be pass interference. The penalty is 15 yards from the

161

spot of the snap and an automatic first down. But in the heat of a game, the receiver cannot depend upon an official seeing the interference. So, you battle for the ball; it is *yours*! But you have to remember that the defensive man is convinced that the ball is *his* property! There is often rugged contact when the receiver and the defender are both going after the ball. You, the receiver, must hang in there and give it all you have.

A receiver who runs deep pass patterns especially must do everything he can to avoid being held up at the line of scrimmage. Otherwise he will not be able to get downfield far enough in time to catch the pass. If you are a wideout, on plays when you are not likely to be receiving a pass, you should try out moves which you can use when you *are* the receiver. It would be rare indeed to find two defensive men doing exactly the same things to hold you up. What will work on one to free you may fail dismally on another. But you try different moves, study the tactics and reactions of different defensive men, learn their weaknesses. Then you will be ready to evade them on passing plays when you *are* the receiver.

Once you are downfield, using a weave approach in which you vary your moves tends to keep the defensive man from countering them. You approach him at three-quarter speed, running an irregular course. You change direction, moving first to the right, then to the left, then to the right again. This presents the defensive man with the problem of shifting his feet and sometimes causes him to slip or stumble. You begin to weave whenever you are approaching the spot downfield where you expect to catch the ball, but you try to make the defender think each weave is the final cut.

Good receivers always vary their pass patterns. One time they may run down the field weaving back and forth. Another time they may go straight down and then slant toward the middle of the field. But they must be sure

ON SOME PASS PATTERNS WEAVE BACK AND FORTH. VARY YOUR PATTERNS.

CATCH THAT PASS AND GO! GO! GO!

to alert their passer when they are going to run a different route. How frustrating to the passer, receiver, and team when the receiver beats his man, is out in the open behind the defender, and the passer throws the ball just the right distance. But the receiver has run a slant-in pattern and the pass was thrown for a slant-out. A sure touchdown or long gain becomes just a wasted down!

Three things are always in the mind of the top receiver after he has run his pattern, fooled his cover, maneuvered into the open, and caught the ball:

1. Grasp the ball firmly. Tuck it under your arm and clutch it tight.
2. There is likely to be immediate and hard contact. Drop your inside shoulder and be prepared for the tackle.
3. Turn upfield and go with all the drive you have.

One thing more: You must make yourself into a good decoy. On many plays you will not be the primary receiver. The quarterback is probably not going to throw the ball to you. But you should be such a convincing actor that defensive men will be fooled into coming after

you, to cover you. This gives the man who *is*
the primary receiver on the play a better chance
to get open, because fewer defensive men will
be in his area of the field. Also, there is always
the possibility that the primary receiver may
be smothered, may be covered so well that your
passer has to try to pick out a man in the open.
That man might be you if you have been such
a good decoy that you have beaten your cover.

BASICS FOR RECEIVERS

1. Become a sticky-fingered player who catches "anything he can reach."
2. Practice getting away fast from the line of scrimmage and practice tactics to avoid being slowed down by defenders.
4. The ball thrown to you is yours. Go after it and fight for it.
5. Keep your eye on the ball. Look the ball into your hands.
6. If you can't catch the ball, make certain that the defender does not catch it.
7. Practice your pass routes. Vary them. No rule forbids a receiver from adding to his moves.
8. Concentrate so well on catching the ball that there is no room in your consciousness to "hear footsteps."

11
The Quarterback

Any coach will tell you that the quarterback is the very core of his offense. Given a boy who is logical in his thinking, bold in action when boldness is called for, a student of football, confident in his ability and able to inspire confidence in his teammates, a coach knows that he can teach the mechanical skills of quarterback play and help him to become an expert field general.

The quarterback is truly a field general. He must be a player who can take command out on the field, one who knows the strengths of his offense and the weak spots in the defense. He is always aware of his team's position on the field, the score, the down coming up and the yardage needed for a first down, and what playing time remains before the end of the half or the game. Then he decides on the strategy and the plays which he feels are likely to work best.

The quarterback must follow the flow of the game. He must look ahead and make decisions. He tries to go by the careful plans his coach has made for the game. For example, the coach may feel that against a certain team, using ground or running plays and keeping possession of the ball for as many series of downs as possible will work better than using a lot of passing plays. However, the quarterback must know when to make adjustments in the game plans.

It is the duty of every player on the team to know what his job is on each and every play. But in order to know how good his weapons of attack are at all times, the quarterback must know the duties of *each and every player for each and every play*. And upon the modern quarterback depends in large degree the success or failure of the most potent offensive weapon, the forward pass.

In practically all plays run from the T-formation and variations of the T, it is the quarterback who throws the ball when a passing play is called. Occasionally, hoping to surprise the other team, a halfback will take a pitchout from the quarterback and throw a pass. But the quarterback is the passer in most of the passing plays.

QUARTERBACK'S STANCE

Suppose you are a quarterback who is going to throw a pass.

You take your stance immediately behind the center. Your feet should be a little wider apart than the breadth of your shoulders. Your weight is on the balls of your feet, your heels and knees turned in slightly. A comfortable bend of the knees combined with a natural bend at the waist will put you in good position to receive the center's hand-back.

Hold your passing hand, palm facing downward, underneath the center's crotch, where you can apply a slight upward pressure. This will help the center to know where to snap the ball. Your other hand should be relaxed and ready to trap the ball, to help in taking the center's snap.

Some coaches teach that the free or bottom hand should be in contact with the passing hand, with the thumb joints touching. Others teach the quarterback to assume whatever position of hands is most comfortable for him. The main idea is to take the ball smoothly from center and to cut down the chances of mishandling it.

ONE WAY TO GRIP THE FOOTBALL

Many football people agree that passers can be overcoached. There are boys who are natural passers, who grip and throw a football easily and accurately and possess a good strong arm. Even if you have such natural throwing ability, there are three areas in which proper coaching and practice can raise you from a good to a great quarterback: grip, release or delivery, and footwork.

No inflexible rules can be set down about how to grip the football. Some passers prefer to place the tip of their little finger about in the center of the lacing, the other three fingers spread toward the back point of the ball, the thumb toward the belly or underside of the football. But you should hold the oval in whatever manner is most comfortable for you. For example, if your hand is small, you will have to grasp the ball closer to the back point.

169

When it is wet, grip the ball less firmly than when dry. This is because your fingers slip more easily on wet leather. The fingers and the palm jointly control the ball, and if it is wet, you should throw with more palm than fingers.

After you take the snap from center, step back. You hold the ball close to your abdomen, ready to fake a hand-off to a runner, hiding your intention to pass but adjusting your grip preparing to pass. After every fake, you bring the ball again to your stomach. If you keep your forearms touching your hips in a relaxed position, you will be able to hold the football closer to your body and hide it more easily. While faking, your weight is shifted toward the back, not toward the extension of your arms. Hold the football with both hands until you are ready to release it, or fake a release.

In position and ready to throw, you are "set up" to pass. You cock your arm so that the football is no higher than your ear and a little behind it. Your release follows.

If you throw right-handed, you set up with your left foot 12 to 18 inches in front of your right foot, depending on your size. (Left-handed passers would have the right foot for-

ward.) Bend your knees slightly. The main
thing is to maintain solid, comfortable balance.
It is not always possible—since the passer is
sometimes called upon to throw while running
or from an awkward position—but maintaining good body balance is one of the most important factors in throwing an accurate pass.

Another important factor in accurate passing is keeping your eyes on receivers who are
running their patterns. Set up in proper throwing position, you should be able to see a passing
field of 180 degrees.

RELEASING THE BALL

Release the ball with a snap of your wrist. Only rarely does a player find he has a good, natural wrist snap, which is probably why so few players are found who are good natural passers. You can learn the wrist snap, though, through drill and practice.

Ready to make a quick, accurate pass to a receiver who has worked into the open, you cock your arm and throw the ball overhand "off your right ear." (Remember, a left-handed passer throws off his left ear.) Except when you are unable to release the ball because of pressure from rushers, or when you are out of the protective pocket and scrambling, you step *toward* the intended receiver onto the foot opposite your throwing arm as you throw. The pass will be more accurate, and in case it is intercepted, you will be going in the right direction to tackle the interceptor.

Proper footwork is as important to the quarterback as grip and delivery. Before you actually pass the ball, you must know the spot from which you intend to throw it. Your teammates who are responsible for forming the protective pocket in front of you should know it too. They realize that you have only a limited time in which to throw, and they will try to give you

protection for that time. Of course, if the protection breaks down, and defensive players are
charging toward you, you *can* leave the pocket
and "scramble," run to get clear of them so
that you can get your pass away. Footwork—
dodging, twisting, sidestepping—is all-important to successful scrambling.

The drop-back passer moves straight back at
least 7 yards from the line of scrimmage, sets
up as quickly as he can, and stays in the pocket
whenever he can. Of course this does not apply
to the quarterback who is going to roll out to
use the option pass. When a quarterback runs
out toward one flank or the other, as though
he is starting a sweep, he is said to roll out. This
particular play gives him a choice—option. He

THIS
QUARTERBACK
CAN
REALLY
SCRAMBLE!

can continue to carry the ball himself to try to pick up yardage or he can throw a pass if he spots a receiver open.

Protective blockers still do their best to keep a pursuing defender from ruining the play by tackling the quarterback from behind, but the major blocking effort is frequently aimed at clearing the path for the quarterback as a ball carrier.

There is no other phase of offense that needs more close attention, coaching, and practice than passing. Here are some pointers that will help you to become a better passer.

1. Take the center's hand-back and step off with the foot most comfortable to you in starting to set up. If you are a right-handed passer, you will probably feel more comfortable stepping off on your right foot.
2. After faking with the football, hide it as you go back and set up.
3. Move back at least 7 yards on drop-back passes and set up fast.
4. Get into position to throw. Be under control yourself and have the football under control.

5. Look straight ahead, but cover 180 degrees of the field where your receivers are maneuvering.

6. Know where the protective pocket is going to be and stay in the pocket when you throw.

7. Arm cocked, ball ear-high, step toward the receiver to whom you are going to release the ball. Step forward on the foot that is opposite your throwing arm. It is awkward to throw off the "wrong foot."

8. Avoid throwing interceptions. "Eat the football" or heave it out of bounds in the direction of a receiver if you can't find a man open.

9. Know your receivers and the pass patterns they run.

10. Learn which players on the other team are the strong and which the weak pass defenders. Then put pressure on the weak man by throwing the ball more often to the man on your team he is covering.

LOOK STRAIGHT AHEAD, BUT COVER 180 DEGREES OF THE FIELD

176 The passing game may provide the greatest potential for quick long gains and touchdowns. But every quarterback knows that unless his team has a strong running attack too, the defense will easily contain the passing game. Part of a running game is the exchange of the football from one back to another. A quarterback must know how to hand off the ball smoothly to his backs and to fake hand-offs.

HAND-OFF

First of all, the quarterback must know well each of the backs to whom he is going to hand off the ball. He must know the back's speed, his strong and weak points, his steadiness or un-steadiness at taking hand-offs.

The quarterback must know the alignment of the defense. If they look as if they are going to rush him, he will pivot away from the de-fense or may have to take a step for position before handing off.

You make your target the far hip of the back to whom you are going to hand off. There must be absolutely no delay in the exchange. It must be very fast. You try to make the hand-off with the same motion you would use if you were dealing cards quickly.

As a beginning quarterback, keep in mind that some backs take the ball with more cer-tainty than others. Generally your first concern is to place the football where your back can most easily grasp it, at the time he is in position to take the exchange. If you use one hand to control the movement of the football and the other to guide it into the "pocket," the "bas-ket" of the back's arms, hands, and abdomen, there will be less chance of a fumble on the hand-off.

Faking a hand-off is very important too. You must always remember to carry out your fakes and make them as real-looking as possible. You should try to go through exactly the same motions you use when you actually hand off the ball.

A quarterback must master the mechanical skills of passing and handing off the football. But as we said earlier, he must be a leader and a student of the game too. Smartness and quickness and the ability to get eleven players to work together as a team are hallmarks of quarterbacks of successful teams. It is a must that the quarterback win and keep the confidence of his teammates. Every member of the team must be *convinced* when his quarterback calls a play that it will *go!*

The quarterback must know offensive play in all its aspects, particularly the system of offense his coach teaches. Of course, it takes time and experience to acquire excellence in calling plays for any offense. Your coach will supply the plays and help you decide when to call them.

The good quarterback works according to plan, within the game plan provided by his coach, but also to "set up the defense." This means that he may run several plays inside the

tackle, for example, to lull the defense into
thinking he has no "outside" attack. Then he
surprises them with a sweep or a reverse, plays
in which the runner goes around the end of
the line instead of through the middle.

When he finds that he can set up the defense
so that a certain play will work, he does not
use it again and again to a point where the defense knows what to expect and smears it. On
the other hand, he does not save up a play that
works well until it is too late in the game to
use it.

Many young quarterbacks find a play that
makes fine yardage, then give it up as though
they are afraid the defense will get on to it.
The other team may get so far ahead on the
scoreboard that you can't go for the sure-gainer
because you must play "catch-up football"—
gamble on long passes. Mix up your plays, use
different kinds of plays to keep the defense
guessing. But when you find that a certain play
works, when a situation arises again that is
similar, use your sure-gainer.

On the field the quarterback is the coach of
the team, or at least he is the coach's repre-
sentative. Even coaches who call a lot of the
plays from the side lines want their field gen-
erals to have and use initiative. One coach told

this story to show how important it is that a quarterback be able to think and act on his own.

"We were in a tough, tight ball game against our traditional rival," he said. "Late in the fourth quarter we were ahead by two points and battling to hang on to the lead. We knew we had to keep the ball away from our opponents because they had a fine field-goal kicker.

"My regular quarterback was belted hard and he fumbled the ball. We were lucky to recover it on our own 6-yard line. The boy was knocked woozy. The clock showed just under two minutes left to play. It was second down and we had 17 yards to go for a first down. I talked to my reserve quarterback before he went into the game.

"Take no chances," I told him. "Keep the ball yourself, don't risk another fumble by a hand-off or pitchout. Squeeze that ball tight after you take the snap, run it into the line for two plays, and then punt!"

The coach stopped and shook his head.

"The boy ran through the center of the line on the first play and reached midfield. He charged through again on the next play and ran 40 yards to the 8-yard line before he was knocked out of bounds. Then he led the team

from the huddle and dropped into the deep
spot of our punt formation. Yes sir, he did. At
this point the kids on the other team were so
confused he could probably have *waltzed* into
the end zone for a touchdown. Instead he
kicked the ball, away over the end-zone
bleachers!"

The coach stood shaking his head, a half-
dazed expression on his face as though he still
could not believe it. He finally said, " 'Run it
into the line for two plays and punt,' I told him.
How can you fault a kid who follows instructions to the letter? But—well, I like my quarterback to think a little on his own!"

"... THEN PUNT!"

College football celebrated 1969 as the Centennial Year and the official centennial game was played between Princeton and Rutgers, as was the very first intercollegiate game back in 1869. Coach John Bateman spoke to a group of New York football writers several days after the game and had this to say about Rich Policastro of Rutgers, a 29–0 victor over Princeton.

"There's no better quarterback in the United States," Bateman told the sports writers. "He sets up real fast, has a very fine release, doesn't get jittery with people coming in on his perimeter, and uses his pocket very well.

"He's a thinking man's quarterback . . . and the team respects him."

Coach Bateman put in capsule form what every coach looks for in a quarterback. If you can lead your team and win their respect and develop the other qualities the Rutgers coach mentioned, you can become a fine quarterback.

182

1. Know your team's plays and the assignment of every teammate on every play.
2. Earn your teammates' respect. Be confident and earn their confidence. You are the boss on the field. Take charge.
3. Know the best play to use against the defense you face *this* game. Remember the plays that work and keep using them, but not so often that the defense knows what to expect.
4. Be aware of how much time is left to play in the game, the number of time outs you have left, the down, your field position, the score, weather and field conditions.
5. Become a student of football, if you are not already, and remain a student of the game.
6. Observe other quarterbacks. Observe and practice anything that will make you a better passer.

OBSERVE OTHER QUARTERBACKS

12
Kicking and Kickers

Every football player knows that the game starts with a kickoff, but most players and many coaches do not appreciate the importance of this first play of the game. Too often a poor play on the kickoff puts a team at a disadvantage during the entire half. The results of kickoff plays may in fact determine the final outcome of a game.

In the sense that the kicking team is giving up possession of the ball to the other team, the kickoff is a defensive play. But it can be a devastating offensive weapon.

Suppose your team has just made a touchdown and the conversion try, but the other team is still ahead in the score. You must kick off, according to the rules, but so little time is left in the game that it looks as though the other team may be able to keep possession of the ball until the clock runs out. You must get

the ball back again in order to mount another scoring drive, and your coach has taught your team a maneuver to use in this situation: the on-side short kickoff.

The rules say that on a kickoff the ball must travel at least 10 yards down the field. Your kicker could of course boot the ball high in the air as usual, but short, close enough to the members of your own team to give you a good chance of recovering it. That would be fine, except that any receiver may signal for a fair catch while a kick is in flight. A smart and alert player on the receiving team might well give the fair-catch signal. This would mean that no member of your team, the kicking team, would be allowed to touch him or the ball unless he happened to fumble the catch. **185**

So instead of a high, short kick, your coach has instructed your kicker to boot the ball along the ground for a short distance instead of in the air, hoping that some fast back or end from your team can outscramble a big lineman from the receiving team and gain possession of the ball. The recovery of a kickoff gives the kicking team a great lift in spirits and often they can go on to score and win the game.

You must never forget that the kickoff is a free ball until it is declared dead by an official. A free ball is one that may be recovered by any player, whether he is on the defensive or offensive team. Players sometimes become confused and allow the kicking team to recover the ball in the end zone. They have the mistaken impression that when a kicked ball crosses the goal line it is dead. A free ball recovered in your end zone by an opponent gives his team a *touchdown!*

For kickoffs, coaches like kickers who can boot the ball high and far. You may have talents that will make you a kickoff expert and assure you of a place on the team.

A kickoff differs from a kick for a point after touchdown or for a field-goal try in that the kicker himself places the ball on the ground for the kick. Usually the ball rests on a kick-

STRAIGHT-ON PLACE
KICK FOR KICKOFFS

ing tee, an artificial device that holds the football on end in a molded, sloping depression. But sometimes kickers just place the ball on end in a depression they make in the ground with their heel. Some even lay the ball flat on the ground. No matter what method the kicker prefers, he uses the same techniques when he boots the ball.

There has been a marked increase in the use of the soccer-type kick for kickoff as well as for try-for-point and field goal, but first let's consider the techniques of the straight-on *place kick*.

187

The kicker approaches the ball at a slow run. His steps are timed to bring his run to an end with the nonkicking foot slightly behind the ball and to the side just as the kicking foot begins to swing forward into the ball.

The length of the run depends on the individual kicker. The average is 7–8 yards, but you may feel you gain more momentum with a longer or shorter run. Experiment until you find the distance best suited to you. Then "groove" it by always stepping off that distance before you kick.

The toe of your kicking foot should meet the ball below its midpoint. At the precise instant of contact lock your kicking leg, bring your leg forward in a "pendulum swing," and follow through all the way. This will give the ball an end-over-end upward flight, the sign of a good kickoff.

The ideal kickoff is long enough to reach the end zone—a minimum of 60 yards, since the kickoff is normally made from your 40-yard line—and high enough to give your teammates time to get downfield and be in position to tackle the receiver before he can run it back upfield too far. Coaches are satisfied if the ball carrier is stopped around the 20-yard line. In any case, the height of the kick is important so that the kick can be well covered when the ball falls short of the end zone.

Kickers may use different-length runs, prefer the straight-on kick or the soccer-type kick. But all of them know that timing is the most important factor in kicking. If you have good coordination and a sense of timing, you are a better kickoff prospect than a boy with longer legs and more strength and power than you, but who lacks coordination and timing.

The soccer-style place kick is different from the more common straight-on kick in two important ways. Your 7- or 8-yard run toward the ball is diagonal rather than straight ahead. You approach the ball at an angle, one you feel comfortable with but usually about 45 degrees. And instead of kicking the ball with your toe, you kick it with the instep, the arched middle part of your foot in front of the ankle joint.

LINED UP AND READY FOR THE KICKOFF

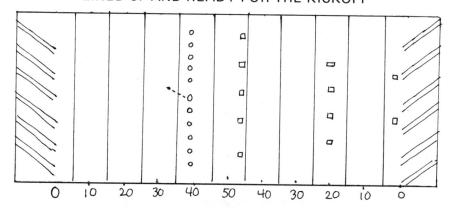

190 Here are some tips from a soccer coach about how to execute the kick.

1. Keep your eyes on the ball.
2. Be sure that when your foot meets the ball, you are balanced.
3. Position your nonkicking foot correctly and lean backward slightly as your foot meets the ball.
4. Follow through fully with your kicking leg.
5. Try to be accurate. Power will come as your timing improves.

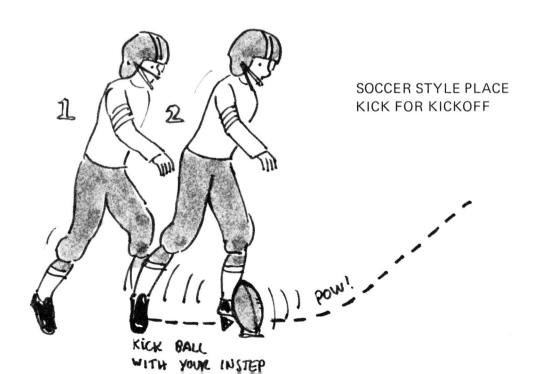

SOCCER STYLE PLACE KICK FOR KICKOFF

1   2

KICK BALL
WITH YOUR INSTEP

POW!

STRAIGHT-ON PLACE KICK FOR FIELD GOALS AND EXTRA POINTS

The techniques of place-kicking for extra points after a touchdown or for a field-goal try are essentially the same as for a kickoff. There are two exceptions, however. The snap from center is taken by another player, a holder, who places the ball in position to be kicked. The ball stands on end and usually slants a bit backward. Second, the run before kicking the field goal or point after touchdown is likely to be no more than a step or two. Getting the kick off quickly over the upstretched hands of charging defensive men is of prime importance.

191

Another kind of kick, the *drop kick*, has in late years almost disappeared from football. It is different from the place kick in that the ball is not held upright on a tee or by a teammate. Instead, the kicker himself drops the football to the ground and kicks it as it begins to bounce up.

One kicker explained that this type of kick is no longer popular because of changes that have been made in the shape of the football. As it became more pointed and streamlined in the interest of better passing, kickers found they could not drop-kick the ball as accurately as before.

The drop kick could be—and occasionally was—used for kickoffs. However, the great advantage of the kick is that a player can get the ball away sooner. A drop kick gives the defense less time to charge through your offensive line and block than a place kick. This advantage makes no difference on kickoffs. Although if you should happen to develop an ability to drop-kick the ball between the uprights and over the crossbar from distances considered to be within field-goal range, you would be welcomed with open arms by any football coach.

The *punt* is different from both the place kick and the drop kick. The ball is not held in place on a tee or by another player. The kicker drops the ball himself, but he kicks it *before* it touches the ground.

The punt is most often thought of as a purely defensive play, but the yards gained by punting are the same length as the yards gained by rushing or passing. Frequently these yards are easier to come by, too—when you have a strong wind at your back, for example.

PUNT

194 There is always a shortage of good punters. Should you discover that you have punting ability, and should you develop that ability until you can boot the ball high, reasonably far, and accurately, your place on the squad is assured. Here are some tips that may help you to become a solid punter.

1. Relax. Your body should be tense only at the instant your foot meets the ball.
2. Stand with your kicking foot slightly ahead of the other foot. Bend your body forward slightly from the hips and flex your knees.
3. Take your stance approximately 13 yards directly behind your center. Your coach may teach you to stand with your arms hanging loose, perhaps swinging slightly until the snapback is made; he may want you to offer a target for the center. As you wait for the snapback, extend your arms. Your hands should be about waist high, your palms facing inward and downward, your fingers pointing forward.
4. Do not fight the ball. Catch it easily with hands relaxed.

5. Move forward on your kicking foot, taking a short step, not more than a foot
or two in length. Then with the nonkicking foot take a natural step forward and
swing your kicking foot into the ball.

6. As you move, adjust the ball in your
hands. The lacing should face upward.
If you kick with your right foot, your
right hand is the one that controls the
ball. Use your other hand to guide and
steady the ball. The long axis of the ball
slants about 15 degrees backward.

DON'T
FIGHT
THE BALL

CATCH
IT WITH
HANDS
RELAXED

7. Release the ball and start your kicking swing as you take the second step forward, the "natural" step. "Lay" the ball on your foot. If you drop it from a height of several inches the wind may blow the ball out of true position. Even with no wind, the ball is out of your control when you drop it toward your foot instead of laying it on your foot. It may land too far to the outside and slice off the side of your foot. Or it may slip too far to the inside. You will then hit it too fully and will bloop the ball, kick it too high and short.

8. Your foot should meet the ball when the ball is a little above knee high. Keep your eyes on the ball until contact is made, then follow through as far as possible with your leg. You should finish your kick with your kicking foot above your head while your weight carries you upward and forward so that you are on tiptoe on the nonkicking foot.

13
Condition

Every candidate for a football team should be examined by a properly qualified physician and approved for play before being issued equipment. Any boy with an organic weakness should not be permitted to play if hard contact might be harmful to him.

The doctor will discover if a bout with rheumatic fever or some other childhood disease has left a heart condition or an incapacity of the lungs or other vital organ which may forbid rough physical activity. Young players should compete only against boys of comparable age, strength, weight, and experience.

Keep in mind that football is a rougher game than baseball or basketball or noncontact sports such as tennis, golf, swimming, and track.

As a football player you must condition your body to absorb heavy blows. Muscles, ligaments, and tendons are called on to stretch quickly and in many different directions. You need to exercise to prepare your body to work efficiently.

It would be foolish to say that any certain exercise will prevent injury, or to set down rules about how many days, weeks, or months an exercise or series of exercises must be done. However, it cannot be emphasized enough that the longer the period exercises are performed *before* rough physical contact, the better shape the body will be in to take physical punishment without breaking down. Always remember, of course, that prolonged exercise may use up muscle strength. Do not *overdo* it.

The wise coach or trainer has his players do warm-up exercises to loosen the muscles, ligaments, and tendons before every practice and before every game. Here is a program of exercises designed to build and strengthen muscles and tendons and ligaments. Your coach may recommend others to you.

Alternate Toe Touch. Holding the knees stiff, bend at the waist and touch the toes of your left foot with the right hand. Then erect and touch the right toes with the left hand in the same manner. Alternate to a count of 40, touching the toes of each foot 20 times.

ALTERNATE TOE TOUCH

Ankle Bounce. Stand with your hands at your sides, with your arms and knees straight. Using only the ankle and calf muscles, jump into the air. Take 20 bounces.

Push-up. Assume a horizontal position, your hands and toes supporting your body. Place your hands on the ground so that they are slightly outside your shoulders, fingers pointing forward. Your arms and body should be perfectly straight. Without letting the stomach sag or your rear end rise, bend your elbows and lower your body until your chin is an inch

199

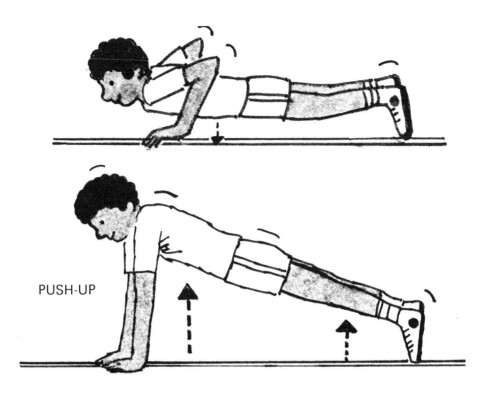

PUSH-UP

or two from the ground. Return to your original position and repeat. Begin with 5 push-ups and gradually increase to 10 or more.

Fingertip Push-up. The position is the same as for the regular push-up, except that the toes and fingertips instead of the toes and hands support the body. Begin with 5 and increase to 10 or more.

Knee-Bend. With your hands on your hips, rotate the body bending from the hips and go into full knee-bend on one count. Straighten on two count. Repeat movement 20 times.

200

Running Backward. From a standing position run slowly backward. Increase your speed as you practice this drill. Try to run in a straight line taking 30 to 50 steps, then turn around and return backward to the point of start.

Running in Place. In a standing position, run to a count of 30 to 50, counting only as one foot hits the ground, either your left or your right.

RUNNING IN PLACE

202   **Side-Straddle Hop.** Stand with your arms at your sides, your feet together. On one count swing your arms over your head and touch your palms together. At the same time jump to spread your feet wide apart. Spring back to your original position on two count. Do the exercise for 50 counts.

Squat Thrust. Stand at attention, your body straight, your arms at your sides. On one count, bend your knees and place your hands on the ground in front of your feet, palms facing down. At a count of two, thrust your legs back so that your body straightens out and your weight is supported by hands and toes. Return to squatting position on three count and to your original position on four. Complete the cycle 10 times.

Trunk Twister. Stand with your hands on your hips, your feet spread comfortably apart. Without moving your feet, twist your body as far to the left as possible, so that your shoulders are in a plane that is nearly perpendicular to your legs. Do this on one count and return to your original position on two. Twist to your right on three and come back to your original position on four. Complete the cycle 10 times.

We are all different in countless ways, but most of us would benefit by paying attention to a few simple things.

1. The body needs regular rest and nature provides a resting period we call sleep. We need at least 8 hours of sleep per day.
2. Your body is your "house," your "machine." Keep it clean as your home or a piece of machinery is kept clean.
3. Eat three meals a day—no more. Give your stomach and digestive system a rest between meals.
4. The food you eat is the fuel your body uses to give you energy. Chew your food thoroughly to prepare it for maximum use as fuel.

EAT ONLY THREE MEALS A DAY

Drink enough water

5. Your body requires a lot of water to flush wastes from your system. Drink enough water. Many experts say you need at least 8 glasses a day.

6. Don't smoke. Aside from the bad effects smoking may have on your heart, and that cigarettes are linked with cancer, smoking is certainly no good for your wind. An athlete needs his lungs working at full capacity; smoking irritates membranes of the throat and lungs and lessens breathing efficiency.

7. Drinking anything with an alcoholic content is even worse than smoking for an athlete.

8. Avoid any use of drugs not prescribed by a physician as medication for an ailment. Avoid such drugs as marijuana, LSD, and other "trip" drugs as you would avoid a crippling disease. Pep pills are not for athletes.

9. Whether you take coffee, tea, or cocoa
   is something that you must decide for
   yourself. They all are stimulants and
   habit-forming to some degree. They may
   do no great harm, but they probably do
   not contribute to maintaining top physical condition.

If you have ever worked hard to get and stay
in good physical condition, you know that it
requires steady effort and sacrifices. There is
no such thing as instant condition, nor any
simple way to become an instant star.

One boy, brought to a southern university
as a freshman flanker, "had it all," as his coach
said. "He had size, speed, great hands, and
coordination, but he lacked one very essential
thing. After our third practice he came to me
and handed me his equipment. He said, 'All
this practice and work is not for me. Making
the team just isn't worth it.'"

Call it will, spirit, pride, morale, persever-
ance, or whatever you like—the good football
player must condition himself to be tough
mentally as well as physically. Every football
coach welcomes the boy so determined to *play*
that playing any one position is secondary to
playing somewhere.

Officials' Signals

Whether you are acting as captain and will be consulted by officials when penalties are called or are simply a spectator, you should know the signals that officials give for infractions of the rules and to keep the game moving.

There are some differences in penalties for various infractions according to pro rules, college rules, and high school rules, but essentially the officials' signals are very much standardized. The signals illustrated in the following pages are National Alliance signals, which are used by officials working games played under National Alliance rules. These rules were adopted by National Federation of State High School Associations and are used almost universally by Pop Warner leagues, Little League football organizations, and other leagues for boys.

Ball ready for play

Clipping, 15 yards

Crawling, 5 yards

Dead ball

Delay of game or encroachment on neutral zone, 5 yards

First down

Grasping opponer face protector, yards

Illegal formation, position, or procedure. Illegal forward handing, 5 yards

Illegal forward pass, 5 yards, down counts

208

Holding or illegal use of hands or arms by the offense, 15 yards; by the defense, 5 yards and automatic first down for offensive team

Illegally kicking or batting a loose ball, 15 yards

Illegal motion or shift, 5 yards (Official uses both hands for illegal shift.)

Ineligible receiver downfield on pass, 15 yards

209

Incomplete forward pass; no play or no score; penalty declined

Intentional grounding of the ball on forward-pass play, 5 yards and loss of down

Loss of down

Officials' timeout

Offside or violation of free-kick rules, 5 yards

Pass interference by offense, 15 yards and down counts; by defense, automatic first down for offensive team at point of infraction

Personal foul, 15 yards

Roughing the kicker, 15 yards and an automatic first down, or running into the kicker, 5 yards and an automatic first down

Safety

Start the clock

Timeout

Touchdown, field goal, or successful conversion after touchdown

Unsportsmanlike conduct, 15 yards

212

Glossary

New terms come into the language of football as occasions for their use come into being. Sometimes these terms are permanent; sometimes they are short-lived. This glossary contains mostly the terms that have endured.

Back judge—The official who operates on the side of the field opposite the *linesman.* His position varies according to the play. He may stand a short distance behind the line of scrimmage or he may be several yards downfield. He assists the linesman in watching for encroachment of the neutral zone and players who are off-side. He helps the umpire to detect illegal use of hands or holding, especially during pass plays or kicks. He assists the referee on forward and lateral passes behind the line and in watching for false starts which might draw the other team off-side. He knows eligible pass receivers. He marks where the ball goes out of bounds on plays within his range on his side of the field. Another of his duties is to notify the home team when it is time to return to the field during intermission between halves. **213**

214 **Ball carrier**—A player in possession of the ball who is trying to advance it toward his opponents' goal by carrying it.

Batting—Striking the ball intentionally with the hand or arm. It is legal for any player who is eligible to touch a forward pass to bat the ball while it is in the air. It is legal to bat the ball in attempting to block a scrimmage kick. Other cases of batting a free ball are illegal and carry a penalty of 15 yards.

Block—The use of the body to stop the progress of an opponent. A player who throws a block to obstruct an opponent becomes a *blocker*. Restrictions on the use of hands and arms in blocking must be observed.

Clipping—A block in which a player throws his body across the back or legs of an opponent other than the runner. Blocking from behind in close line play—in a rectangular area 4 yards on either side of the spot where the snap was made to start the play and 3 yards behind each scrimmage line —is not considered clipping. Blocking from behind anywhere outside this area, in the open field, *is* considered clipping and is subject to a penalty of 15 yards from the spot of the foul.

Counter play—One in which the ball carrier runs against the apparent flow of the play. That is, the play looks as though it is going to the left side of the field. Blockers and fakers start moving in that direction, but the eventual ball carrier goes to the right.

Crawling—The ball carrier attempts to advance the ball after part of his body other than his hands or feet has touched the ground. The penalty is 5 yards. This call depends upon the judgment of an official and is rarely made, since officials do not like to penalize the aggressive ball carrier who keeps his feet driving forward, trying to gain every possible inch.

Dead ball—A ball that is not in play. The ball is dead during the brief period between downs, when it goes out of bounds, and when it has been "killed" by an official's whistle. Nothing can legally happen to a dead ball that affects a team's possession of the ball or their position on the field. (See also *live ball* and *loose ball*.)

Delay of game—Any team failure, player failure, or conduct on the part of a coach or team attendant which causes a team not to be ready for play within the specified time. Also any action that unduly prolongs the game. The penalty is 5 yards.

Double foul—Occurs when both teams commit fouls and the penalties offset each other.

Down—The unit of play. The action that starts with the snap from center, or a free kick, and continues until the ball becomes dead.

Drop kick—A kick in which the ball is dropped to the ground by the kicker, and is kicked just as it rises. (See also *place kick* and *punt*.)

Encroachment—Being in or beyond the neutral zone after the ball is ready for play but before the snap. The man who is making the snap has the right to be over the ball and will not be penalized for encroachment. The penalty is 5 yards.

End zone—The area that is between the goal line and the end line and that extends from side line to side line.

Fair catch—A catch of a kicked ball in which the receiver is protected from being tackled, but forfeits the right to advance the ball. One arm must be raised above the head to signal a fair catch.

Field goal—A ball that is place-kicked or drop-kicked from scrimmage—or a free kick other than a kickoff or punt following a safety—over the crossbar and between the uprights of the opponent's goal post. A ball that passes directly over either upright counts as a successful field goal. A field goal scores 3 points.

Field judge—The official who is primarily responsible for covering kicks from scrimmage, forward passes that cross the defensive goal line, and all loose balls out of range of the umpire, back judge, and linesman. He is also responsible for the supervision of timing, keeping the official time himself when there is no stadium clock or when the clock becomes inoperative. He assists other officials in making decisions about whether players are out of bounds, and covers the reception or interception of passes and recoveries of fumbles in his range.

Flow—The direction in which most backs start

moving after the ball is snapped. If the play is **217** directed toward the left side of the field, the flow is to the left. If the play is going toward the right side, the flow is right.

Forward pass—A ball thrown toward the opponent's goal. Only one forward pass is usually thrown in any play although rules do not prohibit more than one pass being made *behind the neutral zone.* Any forward pass thrown from beyond the line of scrimmage is an illegal forward pass.

Foul—Any infraction of a rule that carries a penalty.

Free ball—Except for a forward pass, a kicked ball that crosses the opponent's goal line, or a punt that has not been touched by a member of the receiving team, a ball that is in play and that is not in possession of a player.

Fumble—Loss of possession of the ball by a player, except when he hands the ball off, passes it, or kicks.

Goal line—A line which separates the end zone from the field of play. This line must be crossed or reached with any part of the ball on, over, or above it to score a touchdown or safety.

Half—The first and second periods of a football game and the third and fourth periods of a football game.

Holding—Using hand(s), arm(s), or leg(s) to grasp or encircle an opponent who does not have the ball. Offensive holding carries a 15-yard penalty. Defensive holding is penalized only 5 yards, but the foul also gives the offensive team an automatic first down.

Huddle—Gathering in a group, usually in a circle, although the huddle may be any shape, to decide on strategy and signals for the upcoming down.

Hurdling—Jumping with both feet or both knees foremost, or attempting such a jump, over a player on the line of scrimmage. Jumping over a player who is on his feet in the open field is also hurdling. This is a personal foul and the penalty is 15 yards from the spot of the foul.

Illegal forward pass—A pass thrown forward from beyond the line of scrimmage; a pass which is intentionally thrown to the ground; a pass batted, caught, or muffled by an ineligible receiver; a pass made after team possession of the ball has changed during a down.

Inbounds—Any place on the playing field between the side lines and end lines. *Inbounds lines* are the lines crossing the yard-mark lines parallel to the side lines. Players and officials commonly refer to these inbounds lines as "hash marks."

Intentional grounding—When the ball is intentionally thrown to the ground in a forward pass play to avoid a loss of yardage.

Interception—Occurs when a player of the defending team catches a pass (gains legal possession of the ball) before a player of the passing team.

Intermission—The period between the end of the second quarter (first half) and the beginning of the third quarter (second half). In college games the intermission is 15 minutes long. High school teams take an additional 3 minutes for warm-up activity.

Kickoff—A *place kick* made from the 40-yard line of the kicking team (unless a penalty moves the ball backward or forward) that starts the game, starts the second half, and puts the ball in play after a touchdown or field goal. The ball may be placed on the ground or on a kicking tee. A *drop kick* may be but is rarely used instead of a place kick on a kickoff.

Lateral—A pass that is also known as a backward pass. The ball may be thrown backward and away from his goal line or parallel to his goal line by any player to a teammate at any time.

Line of scrimmage or **scrimmage line**—Actually there are two lines of scrimmage, one for the offensive and one for the defensive team. Each is an imaginary line that runs across the field parallel to the goal line and through the point of the football that is nearest each team's goal line when the ball is placed in position and ready for play. The offensive team must have at least seven players on or within a foot of their line when the ball is put in play by a scrimmage down. They may have more than seven if desired. The defensive team may position any number of players on or behind their scrimmage line but they cannot be in advance of their scrimmage line before the ball is snapped. In common usage, football people speak of "playing in the line" or "hitting the line" as meaning players who line up on or within a foot of the scrimmage line as contrasted to players who line up in the backfield behind the line of scrimmage.

Linesman—The official who operates on the side of the field, which side being designated by the referee. He is also referred to as headlinesman. He is not to be confused with a "lineman" which is a term used to describe a player, such as a guard or tackle, who lines up on or within a foot of the line of scrimmage. A primary responsibility of the linesman is to determine if players are offside. The linesman also supervises the mechanics of his chain crew and down-box operator. He covers runners and passes and kicks on his side of the field, deciding when they are in or out of bounds.

Live ball—A ball that is in play during a down. (See also *dead ball* and *loose ball.*)

Loose ball—A ball that has been kicked, fumbled, or passed is loose until it becomes dead or until a player has possession, whichever happens first. Possession occurs when a player legally controls the ball.

Man-in-motion—One player in the offensive back-field may be in motion before and as the ball is snapped, providing that his motion is parallel with or toward his own goal. He must remain in the position he lines up in for one second before he starts his motion.

Monster man—A linebacker in some defense formations in which he is "rover," moving laterally, from side to side, in either direction or wherever he senses the point of attack to be.

Multiple foul—Two or more fouls committed by a team on the same play. The offended team captain has the choice of which penalty will be accepted.

Neutral zone—The area between the offensive scrimmage line and the defensive scrimmage line.

Offside—A player is offside when any part of his body is beyond his scrimmage line when the snap occurs or is in advance of his restraining line when a free kick is made.

Out of bounds—A player is out of bounds when any part of him touches anything, other than another player, which is on or outside a side line or end line.

Period—One of four divisions of playing time in a football game, during which a team advances toward one goal. At the end of each period teams change goals. A period is also referred to as a *quarter*. College games are played in 15-minute quarters and high school games in 12-minute quarters.

Personal foul—Striking an opponent with fist, locked hands, forearm, or elbow. Kicking or kneeing another player, tripping, clipping, grasping an opponent's face mask, hurdling, and blocking or tackling or roughing the kicker are also classified as personal fouls.

Place kick—A kick in which the ball is held upright on a tee or held by a teammate.

Punt—A kick in which the kicker drops the ball and kicks it before it touches the ground. This kick is used as a scrimmage kick and may be used as a free kick after a safety. (See also *place kick* and *drop kick.*)

Recovering—Gaining possession of the football after a fumble.

Referee—The official who has general responsibility for and control of the game. The referee is the final authority for the score and has the final decision on all matters not specifically under the jurisdiction of another official. The referee takes position behind the offensive team.

Return kick—A kick made by the player who receives a punt, kickoff, or drop kick. He immediately kicks the ball back to his opponents, or may run several steps and then kick it. This is now very seldom used.

Safety—A score made when the ball becomes dead in the end zone, or over the end line, in possession of a player of the team defending that goal line, when the impetus that carried the ball into the end zone came from the defensive team. A safety scores two points, and the team it is scored against must put the ball in play by a free kick from its 20-yard line.

Scrimmage—The action of play beginning with the center's snap and ending when the ball is dead.

Shift—When two or more players of the offensive team change position *after* lining up at scrimmage and *before* the ball is snapped, without remaining stationary for a full second after the change in position is made. The penalty is 5 yards.

Snap or **snapback**—The action of the center as he hands back or passes back the ball to a player in the backfield.

Tackle—The use of hands, arms, or body by a defensive man to stop the ball carrier.

Timeout—When a play is stopped and the clock is stopped at the request of either team or an official. During each half of a game played in 12-minute quarters, teams may call four time outs. For each half of a game played in 15-minute quarters, they may call 5. No time out may exceed 1½ minutes.

Touchback—Occurs when the ball is put into the defensive team's end zone with the impetus provided by the team attacking that goal, but the ball becomes dead in possession of a defender of that goal. A touchback scores no points. The next scrimmage down starts on the defensive team's 20-yard line and they become the offensive team.

Touchdown—The act of scoring in which the ball

is in possession of a player and is on, above, or over the opponent's goal line and in bounds. A touchdown scores six points and entitles the scoring team to one additional play to try-for-point after touchdown.

Try-for-point—The play allowed after a touchdown in which a team tries to score extra points. A place kick or drop kick over the crossbar and between the uprights of the goal post scores one point. Present college and high school rules allow the ball to be run or passed, and if the play is completed in the end zone, two points are scored.

Umpire—The official who is primarily responsible for player action in the line and for action that takes place between him and the play. He is positioned behind the defensive line, close enough to it (usually 5 to 8 yards) to be able to detect any fouls. The umpire keeps a record of the winner of the toss, the number of time outs charged to each team, and all scores.

Unsportsmanlike conduct—The rules say that no player, coach, or team attendant shall act in an unsportsmanlike manner during any period of play or intermission. This includes any act an official deems unsportsmanlike, such as using insulting language or gestures that breed ill-will.

Wideout—A pass receiver who most often runs his patterns wide and deep, toward the side line far down the field. The term is usually applied to split ends and flankers.

Index

About the Author

C. Paul Jackson's books for young people grow out of his long-time interest in sports and in boys. For many years, Mr. Jackson was on the faculty of the Lincoln Junior High School in Kalamazoo and officiated at athletic contests in southwestern Michigan schools. He is the author of *How to Play Better Baseball*, *How to Play Better Basketball*, *Little Leaguer's First Uniform*, and *Rose Bowl All-American*.

Mr. Jackson received his A.B. degree and teaching certificate from Western Michigan College of Education and an M.A. degree from the University of Michigan.

About the Illustrator

Leonard Kessler is a writer and illustrator of children's books as well as a designer and painter.

Mr. Kessler was born in Akron, Ohio, but he moved to Pittsburgh at an early age. He was graduated from the Carnegie Institute of Technology with a degree in fine arts, painting, and design. Len Kessler enjoys playing the clarinet and is an avid football fan. He loves the Pittsburgh Steelers! Mr. Kessler lives in New City, New York.